Remembering

GARRETT

Remembering

GARRETT

ᔐ

ONE FAMILY'S BATTLE WITH A CHILD'S DEPRESSION

Esteem,

UNITED STATES SENATOR
GORDON H. SMITH

CARROLL & GRAF PUBLISHERS
NEW YORK

REMEMBERING GARRETT
One Family's Battle with a Child's Depression

Carroll & Graf Publishers
An Imprint of Avalon Publishing Group, Inc.
245 West 17th Street
11th Floor
New York, NY 10011

AVALON
publishing group incorporated

Copyright © 2006 Gordon Smith

First Carroll & Graf edition 2006

This memoir is a product of the author's recollections and is thus rendered as a subjective accounting of events that occurred in his/her life. All photos are part of the author's collection.

Library of Congress Cataloging-in-Publication Data is available.

ISBN-10: 0-7867-1762-9
ISBN-13: 978-0-78671-762-0

9 8 7 6 5 4 3 2 1

Book design by Maria E. Torres

Printed in the United States of America
Distributed by Publishers Group West

To Sharon Lankford Smith
Garrett's angel mother, his "awesome mom"

CONTENTS

When I was a child, I spoke as a child, I understood as a child, I thought as a child: but when I became a man, I put away childish things.

For now we see through a glass, darkly; but then face to face: now I know in part; but then shall I know even as I am known.

And now abideth faith, hope, charity, these three; but the greatest of these is charity.

1 Corinthians 13:11–13

PREFACE

By United States Senator Edward Kennedy
and United States Senator Orrin Hatch

T his sensitive, intelligent, and emotionally moving book by one of our warmest and most likable colleagues in the United States Senate is the story of two exceptional parents who loved and lost, who cared for and now deeply mourn, their son.

Remembering Garrett is powerful not only because of its vivid description of the many highs and lows and sudden sharp curves in the life of Garrett Smith but due to the continued and heroic efforts of his parents to deal with the mental illness that ultimately took Garrett's life.

Psychiatrists call the condition that afflicted Garrett manic depression, or bipolar disorder. It's little understood, and sadly for Garrett and his family, the modern scientific revolution has not yet crossed this frontier in medicine. But it will, if we keep at it.

Parents in every community face the immense challenge of helping family members and friends suffering from this heart-wrenching illness. So do nations. Some of the most important leaders in history have suffered from manic depression, among them Winston Churchill, the great British statesman, and Abraham Lincoln, one of our finest presidents. We think as well of the renowned composer Robert Schumann and the explorer Merriwether Lewis.

In Garrett Smith's case, his days were filled with sudden shifts, from supreme elation to ineffable sadness, from exuberant self-confidence to intense self-doubt. He waged his daily battle for twenty-one extraordinary years, until the mood swings inexorably led him to end his life.

At his peaks, he had it all. He could transport all who knew him, especially his parents, into worlds of happiness and joy. In his valleys, when he was distressed and doubting, suddenly turning inward, he became unreachable.

Yet we also see here that, for a time, Garrett's life was a triumph of faith. During the period when he served his mission for the Church of Jesus Christ of Latter-Day Saints, he found himself fulfilled. Drawing on the strength of his commitment and also sheer willpower, he diligently worked with and cared for others, more than living up to his responsibilities. Throughout those rewarding two years, Garrett was able to stave off the illness that was constantly eroding his well-being.

Gordon Smith's chronicle of love and loss will touch all readers, but most particularly those who themselves have children. In truth, the compelling story of Garrett's struggle and his parents' love for him should help anyone who reads it to become a more concerned and compassionate person.

Such tragedies as Garrett's must be prevented. Thanks to his father, who was inspired by his son's legacy to work for the enactment of landmark mental health legislation in Congress, Garrett is making a difference from beyond the grave. Certainly, we believe his unforgettable story will encourage every person who learns of it to support the search for greater knowledge and more effective remedies. We think God brought Garrett to Gordon and Sharon Smith for precisely that purpose.

We commend this book to the nation because we know it will touch every reader's soul.

PROLOGUE

I can still hear the knock at the door. I can still feel the dread
that filled my heart.

My wife Sharon was frantically calling me to come downstairs. The police were at the door.

It was nearly ten P.M. on September 8, 2003, and I was getting ready for bed and unpacking our suitcase. Sharon and I
had returned to our Bethesda, Maryland, home after attending

a political event on Sea Island, Georgia. But, throughout an otherwise enjoyable time, our anxiety levels had been rising. Our son, Garrett, was turning twenty-two the next morning, and for the past few days we had been trying to reach him at his college in Utah, with no success. Our anxiety grew to alarm when the greeting on his voice mail changed. "This is Smith," came his voice. "I'm not feeling well. Please don't call me anymore!"

Upon hearing Sharon's call, I quickly threw on some clothes, rushed downstairs, and invited two Montgomery County policemen into our home. They asked if there was a quiet place we could sit together. I led them into my den and, once seated around the fireplace, one of them said, "Senator and Mrs. Smith, I don't know how to make this easy, but I have the duty to tell you that your son, Garrett Lee Smith, was found dead in his college apartment. It appears to be a suicide."

Words fail me in trying to adequately describe the crushing weight such a message brought to Sharon and me—or would bring to the parents of any child. Through watery eyes and the sounds of Sharon's sobbing, I exchanged contact information with the officers and showed them out as best I could. As the door closed, shock and numbness held me for a moment above what looked to be the blackest depths of sorrow and failure. Joy vanished and years of striving and achieving now appeared as ashes to me. Success in business, service in church, election to the United States Senate—in an instant, it all seemed meaningless, even vain. I had failed to save my own son. I felt I had failed at my most important and lasting responsibility: that of family, of fatherhood.

After holding on to Sharon for a long time and trying to think, I realized I had to let a few people know of the terrible news that Garrett was gone. I made two phone calls. The first was to my oldest brother, Milan, who, since the death of my parents, had served as a family leader and true friend to me and to our eight other brothers and sisters. I knew I could lean on his strength and wisdom as I buckled under the weight of my life's greatest tragedy. He would bear me up and dust me off as he'd done many times since I was a little boy. I told him what had happened and asked him to let other family members know. I recall little else of the conversation, but I knew instinctively that he would go into action, and attend to legal details with the authorities in Utah.

Then I called Sue Keenom, my executive assistant at the Senate. "Garrett is gone," I said. "He's taken his life. I won't be in this week. I've got to go get my boy, and take him back to Oregon to bury him."

Shocked as she was, Sue set in motion all the Senate office machinery that would help sustain Sharon and me through the suffering and grieving ahead.

For a long time, Sharon and I had seen Garrett struggle with dyslexia, poor self-worth, and descend into dark and dangerous depressions. Recently he'd confessed to us that the thought of suicide had entered his mind, and now that he'd done it, I blamed myself. How had it come to this? Why hadn't I been there more for my son? Why had I spent so much of the past decade running for and serving in public office, in some way trying to save the world, when I should have been concentrating on saving my son? How could I have better helped Garrett love himself as much as Sharon and I loved him? These questions seemed to constitute a perdition of my own making.

Unable to sleep and unable to be of much solace to Sharon, I staggered up to Garrett's room, fell on his bed, clutched his old teddy bears to me and spent a night in hell, crying out to him, screaming at myself, pleading with God for understanding, for forgiveness, for mercy, for the strength to go on.

Since that night, I've received some answers to my questions. They have come slowly, often silently and powerfully, but always with some pain.

This is the story of my son, Garrett. It is the story of the joy he brought to our lives and the challenges he faced. It is the story of how his death changed our lives and my service in the United States Senate. It is the story of how Sharon and I— through sharing Garrett's story very openly and publicly—have found the strength to go on. It is my profound hope that this story will offer guidance to the countless parents who have a child battling mental illness or depression, and solace to those parents who, like us, may have lost a child to those diseases.

In writing this book, in becoming a soldier in the battle against youth suicide, I am violating the last thing Garrett asked of me. He wrote in his suicide note, "Put me in the ground and forget about me."

Forgive me, son, but I cannot forget about you. This is our story.

ONE

ⵋ

Any boy's story really begins with his mother, so I'll start with Sharon Lankford. In the fall of 1973, I reenrolled as a sophomore at Brigham Young University in Provo, Utah, after completing a two-year mission in New Zealand for the Church of Jesus Christ of Latter-Day Saints. I hadn't been at school long when I saw her and even today, after thirty years of marriage, my heart swells when I remember the moment. We were both standing in front of a dormitory complex near the BYU campus, ironically trying to rekindle romances from our teenage years. I loved her at first sight and I still do, but now for more than just her physical beauty. Before long, I fell in love with her compassion for others, her dedication to duty, with how determined she was to always better herself.

Our courtship was awkward at first because our backgrounds were so different. She was a valley girl from Sepulveda, California. Her father, Willis E. Lankford—Lanky, as he was called—was a big, tall, handsome marine who'd fought in the South Pacific in World War II. He caught a desperate case of malaria while on Guadalcanal and later, during his convalescence at a military hospital in Seattle, he met a WAVE named Vivian Dawn Fountain who bore a striking resemblance to Vivien Leigh. Naturally, they fell in love.

At war's end they married and moved to Southern California, where Lanky joined the Hollywood Division of the Los Angeles Police Department. Lanky and Dawn—as she was known—settled into the middle-class suburbia of the San Fernando Valley and had three children: James, Sharon, and Carla. Their childhood bordered between comfortable and Spartan. Sharon still recalls watching with envy as other children, whose parents could afford it, enjoyed the pony ride at the shopping center near their home. (Today, after dinner at the White House, an audience with the Pope, or a visit with royalty in a foreign palace, Sharon can still be heard to say, "That was a pretty good pony ride!")

Religion wasn't a part of daily life at the Lankfords. Lanky was born a Baptist but was not devout. Dawn, though born in Utah, had long been estranged from the Mormon faith of her childhood. The Lankfords' son Jimmy was prone to serious juvenile delinquency and ran away from home at an early age. His adult life would be troubled, as well, and Sharon and I would try to be helpful by occasionally sending him money. I never was to meet him before he passed away a few years ago.

Warm, friendly people, the Lankfords were part of a large social circle of veterans and law enforcement colleagues. Tragically for the family, alcohol was at the center of that circle. Sharon was a young teenager and Carla in elementary school when their mother died from liver failure. Before she died, she urged Sharon to seek out the faith of her Mormon ancestors and to qualify herself to attend Brigham Young University. I never knew Dawn Lankford, but I am eternally grateful that she put her daughter on a path that led her to me.

At age sixteen, Sharon became a guardian to her little sister and a caregiver to her father. She cooked the food, washed the clothes, cleaned the house, saw to the homework, got her sister to bed, and waited for her father to come home at night. Because she had to, Sharon became a great woman while still a girl, and she dreamed of a day that she could marry someone whose schedule and income could provide her with a stable, predictable future. A dentist, she imagined. When she took me for a husband, her life unfolded quite differently from her dreams.

My upbringing, on the other hand, was idyllic, even privileged. I'm the eighth of ten children. My father, Milan D. Smith, was a very busy, brilliant, and accomplished man. He prospered in all that he did—as a food-processing entrepreneur in Oregon; in public service in Washington, D.C., where he worked in the highest levels of the Eisenhower Administration, in leading the National Canners Association, in real estate, in finance, and in civic endeavors for Rotary International and the Boy Scouts of America. He was a man always on the move, and moving in high places.

And yet, if ever I needed him, as he proved many times, my father would stop for me. He and I shared an unusually close relationship. We had an intuitive understanding of each other, an appreciation that in fact grew out of tragedy.

Around the time I was born, Dad owned a single-engine Air Coupe plane that he loved to fly around the country to the many meetings he had to attend. At some point, a mechanic accidentally left his lunch bag in the engine compartment. Who knows how long it was in there, but it went unnoticed until the day Dad tried to take off out of Bend, Oregon. The bag got tangled with the airplane's carburetor, causing the engine to stall. The Air Coupe lost speed and the plane, with Dad at the controls and my mother next to him, plummeted to earth. Dad banked the plane so it hit in such a way that my mother suffered only broken ribs, but in doing so, he took the brunt of the impact on himself. The right side of his face was smashed and his right eye destroyed.

Years later he'd say he had "made a greater impression on Bend, Oregon, than any living man." It was a brave joke, but it belied the severity of what happened to him. My handsome and dashing Dad was damaged physically and psychologically, and his recovery was painful and long, even life-long. Mother always contended that I, as the infant at home, became a focus of his attention and affection, and crucial to his recovery. Day after day and surgery after surgery, he would push me about Pendleton in a baby pram, renewing his health and regaining his hope. I have no memory of these tender times, but I have never forgotten the strong cords of love that tied us together, father and son. Nor have I forgotten a central lesson of his life—that when you get knocked down, it's imperative that you get up.

My mother, Jessica Udall, was a saint. A first cousin to Arizona political legends Stewart Udall and the late Morris Udall, she was busy like my father, but always beautiful and fit, friendly and engaging, talented in music and gifted in home-making. In between herding us to school, sports, Boy Scouts, and whatever else was demanded by her large brood, she found time to read to us from the best books and teach us piano. I honestly don't know how she did it. My mother was a marvel.

Religious activity was a central feature of Smith family life. Meals always started with a blessing. Family prayer and scripture reading were common, obedience to church standards was expected, and church attendance was required. And yet, the religious environment my parents created for us never felt compulsory to me, but invitational. They taught us correct principles—integrity, honesty, charity, morality, and more—and hoped we'd govern ourselves. For the most part, we did. And when we didn't, Mom and Dad always found out. In addition to his business and civic responsibilities, Dad was, throughout my adolescent years, the Stake President, which in the Mormon hierarchy is equivalent to an archbishop in a Catholic archdiocese. He had vast responsibilities over the mid-Atlantic region, and though we weren't public figures in a political sense, we certainly were in the Latter-Day Saint community. If we ever strayed from the straight and narrow, it was noticed and reported. My most enduring memory of Mother is of her seated at the church organ, playing hymns for the congregation, Sunday after Sunday, year after year, occasionally throwing an eagle's glare at us to guarantee suitable reverence. In truth, we were usually behaving because fooling around in church could result in no dessert at dinner—a severe punishment to be avoided at all costs. Along with everything else, Mom made delicious desserts!

And so I brought that enviable childhood with me to BYU and met someone who I'd probably never have met anywhere else, so great were the differences in our lives. I chased Sharon until she caught me and eighteen months after that first meeting in front of the dorm, we became engaged. We were married on June 6, 1975, and my love for her grows with each passing year.

TWO

As I finished my bachelor's degree at BYU, we made plans to move to Los Angeles. I would attend Southwestern University School of Law, Sharon planned to continue teaching second grade, and we'd very quickly start having children. Sharon graduated from BYU cum laude in Elementary Education; by nature and nurture she was very maternal, and coming from a large family myself, I hoped that we would have many children. Settling into life in Southern California, we both looked forward to Sharon becoming pregnant as soon as possible. But it didn't happen right away.

And then months went by and it still didn't happen. Some Sunday evenings I would find Sharon in tears at the prospect of another week's work with no baby in sight. She wanted to stay home. She wanted children. Months turned into years and after too much of this sad longing, we finally sought professional help at a Westwood, California, fertility clinic. There were tests, thermometers, charts, calendars, drugs, and even surgeries, until the doctors told us that it was so unlikely we'd ever have children together, we should consider adoption. The news struck me hard. As much as it was—I thought—the end of a dream, it was a challenge to my ego and a test of my heart. Did I have enough love to make another's child my own? After much contemplation and prayer, I concluded that I did, and that I should. For her part, Sharon was enthusiastic from the beginning, and after a number of interviews and home visits by social workers, we were approved for adoption. Then we waited some more.

In May 1979 we were still waiting. I graduated from law school, and accepted a position as a law clerk to Justice H. Vern

Payne of the New Mexico Supreme Court so we asked that our adoption paperwork be transferred to LDS social services in New Mexico. We loaded up a U-Haul and set out for Santa Fe. The best Christmas present we could ever imagine finally arrived that December, when we were given an appointment to pick up our new baby girl in Albuquerque.

I'll always remember Sharon's face when that infant was placed in her arms. She glowed with the pure joy and contentment of a mother's love. When Sharon handed the baby to me, any doubts I'd ever had disappeared. At that moment I knew that my heart was big enough, too. Having adopted three children over the years, I now realize that to have a new baby in your home for an hour is to have them in your heart forever.

We named the baby Brittany Anne Smith and she became the center of our lives. With her big blue eyes, button nose, and bald head topped with a little blonde curl, she looked a lot like the cartoon character Tweety Bird and I could hardly wait to get home after each day's work at the court to see if she had changed while I was gone. We applauded when she rolled over and encouraged her first steps as if she'd invented walking. I paraded her everywhere, to neighbors and friends, to colleagues and jurists, and family far and wide so they could hear the clap of her hands and see her big, toothless grin. Everyone adored Brittany and we loved her more than life itself. Our wait was over and the wait had been worth it.

When my clerkship ended, we had to decide where to establish a residence and raise our family. Though I had passed the New Mexico bar exam and had really fallen for that beautiful state, especially Santa Fe, the job offer I'd been hoping for from a law firm there never came through. Time for Plan B. We didn't have to think that long to settle on Arizona, a state we both were drawn to, and home to my mother's family. Indeed, many of my siblings had made Arizona their home too and even my parents had retired in Mesa. The Udalls have a saying that there are more Udalls in Arizona than You-alls in Texas, and it's not much of an exaggeration; my Udall cousins run into the hundreds and the extended genealogy goes into the thousands.

Being close to family wasn't the only thing that drew us to Arizona, though. My Udall family legacy had loomed large in my mind since I was young. In a sense, the Udalls are to Arizona what the Kennedys are to Massachusetts. My great-grandfather, David King Udall, was one of the lawmakers who drafted Arizona's constitution when it was admitted to statehood. My grandfather, Jesse A. Udall, was for many years the chief justice of the Arizona Supreme Court. My second cousins, Stewart Udall and Morris Udall, were prominent political leaders in the Democratic party and on the national stage. (Today, I serve in Congress with two of their sons, Representative Tom Udall of New Mexico and Representative Mark Udall of Colorado.) Throughout Arizona, Udalls, both Republicans and Democrats, served at the local, county, and state level in executive, legislative, and judicial capacities. To be born into a Udall home is to be nurtured with the ethic of public service. And, because my parents talked much of political affairs and served amply in public life, I had sometimes thought of running for office one day.

The importance of politics first came to me when I was eight years old. My parents avidly followed the Nixon-Kennedy debates and I watched and learned at their knees, listening to their commentary as the black-and-white television screen flickered in the living room. When Kennedy won the general election, my father finished his service in the Eisenhower administration as assistant secretary of agriculture and cabinet coordinator. But even with a new administration in office, the family would still have ties to the nation's government: Stewart Udall was nominated to serve as Secretary of the Interior in President-elect Kennedy's cabinet.

Though my parents were Republicans, out of what I suspect were pride in, and respect for, my mother's cousin Stewart we attended the Kennedy inauguration. It was cold and clear in Washington, D.C., on January 20, 1961, and it had snowed the night before. Mother bundled us up and Dad drove us toward the Capitol building for an experience that burned itself into my memory: the singing, the Robert Frost poem, the young President and his beautiful wife, his soaring speech, the simple, powerful oath of office, the booming of the distant cannons, the excitement of the parade. It all impressed me as great, even magical in its way, and though very young, I had caught my first case of "Potomac Fever."

So, with one eye on the road to Arizona and the other on my Udall political heritage, I got behind the wheel of yet another U-Haul van for what I felt would be our last Adventure-in-Moving. Sharon, baby Brittany, and I unloaded our old student furniture into a new development located not far from my parents. All our savings had gone into the down payment, so we were determined to live on leverage and love. I passed the Arizona bar exam and hung up my shingle with a Mesa law firm.

We were all set for a long and happy life. And then very quickly I discovered something that I was fortunate to learn so early in my legal career—I didn't like practicing law. Though I'd loved my years in law school and my experience as a judicial clerk, practicing law to me was confining, quite tedious, and awfully confrontational for my restless spirit. I knew I couldn't feel that way for long and prosper as a lawyer. I wanted to be out among people, moving around and making things happen, and I knew deep down that the richest people in the world weren't the ones with the most money, but those who earned their daily bread doing what they loved for families they loved. The law had always been my second career path, anyway. Even before politics, my fondest boyhood hope had been to be like my dad, a food processing entrepreneur.

* * *

My earliest memory in life is of riding in a convertible, sitting on the lap of my grandfather, Albert T. Smith, as Dad drove us the few miles from our Oregon home to the Smith Canning and Freezing Company in Pendleton. My grandfather had founded the company in Utah, but he'd cast his eyes to the rolling hills of northeast Oregon as the perfect place to expand his business of processing peas, corn, carrots, and other vegetable crops.

What I remember most about that day was entering a cold-storage warehouse and feeling the blast of frigid air hit my face. Looking back out of the relative darkness of the warehouse, through row upon row of bins stacked high with frozen peas, I saw my father and grandfather bathed in sunlight, standing by a railcar, no doubt talking family business. I suppose my recollection is so vivid because of the sensory overload of riding in a convertible for the first time and strolling on a hot summer day into a frozen food warehouse. But what really kept that memory alive was the boyhood pride I felt in my family at that moment, and my hope to be part of their heritage and industry.

Kennedy inaugural or not, when I left for New Zealand for my LDS mission—when young Mormon men turn nineteen, they have the opportunity to serve the church for two years as a missionary in another state or country—I had had every intention of coming back to a life in frozen foods. But then a funny thing happened while I was halfway around the world: my father sold the company to my sister, Melanie, and her husband, Dr. Norman R. Jones. Disappointed as I was, I was sincerely happy for them and set aside my boyhood dream of running the family business and set a course for a career in law.

Norman and Melanie made a very bold move by consolidating the business's three small factories into one large one at Weston, Oregon, twenty miles outside of Pendleton. It was a visionary decision, but the debt it created, an oversupply of vegetables, and correspondingly low prices in the industry, made for difficult timing and seven lean years. Luckily Norman was an entrepreneur at heart with a keen eye for real estate development. As their food processing fortunes declined, their real estate assets multiplied.

Suddenly, however, Norman was stricken with leukemia. He died very quickly, leaving my sister a widow with seven young children. And to make matters worse, all their real estate assets served as collateral to their food processing liabilities. Melanie knew that she couldn't run the business while raising her children and asked my father, my brother Milan Jr., who was a gifted business lawyer, and myself to help sort out company and estate matters. Four attempts were made to sell the plant at Weston, but each, for one reason or another, failed to close.

By now I had realized my true feelings about the law, and that my food processing ambitions had never died. Perhaps, I wondered, I could raise the money to buy the company and live my boyhood dream after all? Unfortunately, the only money I had was the equity in our home and in one other piece of real estate. So I went to the man I admired most in the world, my father, to gauge his interest in coming in with me on the deal.

"Son," he replied, "I am too old to do this again, this business is too risky to burden your mother's estate with, and I have too many other children for whom I cannot do the same. If you are determined to do this, you've got to put together a business plan that is fair to your sister and satisfies the bank. I will help you with my mind and my experience, but not with my money."

I *was* determined. I wanted this opportunity as much as I wanted air to breathe. But on the other hand, I didn't want to be my sister's employee. I came up with the following proposal: for half the stock in Jones-Normal Foods I'd sell my real estate and borrow what additional I could, and if I could turn the company around, I'd pay her full book value through a stock redemption for the remaining half, also releasing her real estate assets from bank collateral. She agreed and traveled with Dad and me to Portland, to help sell the agreement to the bankers.

I presented the agreement and my business plan to the men in pin-stripes around the table. Dad backed me with his insightful comments and natural credibility. That, coupled with the fact that Jones-Normal Foods had by now exhausted its net worth, led to the bank president overruling the loan officer's recommendation. He ended the meeting by saying, "Gordon, we're going to extend the company credit for one more season. You've got to turn this around by then or it's over. I believe you can and that you will. I'm counting on you. The whole bank is counting on you."

When I called Sharon in Arizona, bursting with enthusiasm to tell her the news, she asked, logically, "Honey, why did you go to law school if all you really wanted to be was a pea picker in Pendleton?"

THREE

Moving back to the place where I was born filled me with so much anticipation and ambition that I never looked into the U-Haul's rearview mirror. The law and the Arizon border were behind me. Political ambitions also receded in my mind. All I wanted now was to turn around the family business, which I soon renamed Smith Frozen Foods.

Success in a commodity business goes to those who control costs, produce quality, provide superior service, and can meet the price fluctuations of the market. In most years, no matter how hard you work, success is breaking even and holding on until the next year, but in the recessionary times of the 1970s, many vegetable processors couldn't hold on. All those failed companies created low national inventories of frozen vegetables and reduced industry capacity. Add some timely rains and a huge amount of hard work and Smith Frozen Foods was able to achieve a degree of success. Within a few years, Melanie and I had completed the sale and managed to free all her other assets from the market vicissitudes of peas, corn, and carrots. And Sharon, Brittany, and I were as happy and content as three peas in a pod.

Then came another surprise. And we named him Garrett Lee Smith.

* * *

Coming home to Brittany and Sharon each day with my boots dusty and my clothes either splattered with corn juice or stained by green pea vines always felt to me like walking over the threshold of heaven. We'd been blessed with a good life, and both Sharon and I knew in our hearts that we wanted to share that life with a brother or sister for Brittany. We were ready to adopt again, so we asked that the paperwork we'd completed for Brittany's adoption be transferred to the regional church offices in Spokane, Washington. The social worker assigned to our family paid us a call to update our file and warned us that we shouldn't be impatient, as infants available for adoption were becoming increasingly rare. Happy as we were with our nineteen-month-old baby girl, we told him we were content to wait.

It came as a shock when, one month later, we received a call to pick up a newborn baby boy. When we asked, incredulously, what had happened to speed up the process, we were told of a remarkable set of circumstances. The baby had been born in Seattle. As is the practice in all the offices of LDS Social Services, the placement of the child is made only after much thought and prayer, but the social workers in Seattle felt no direction, no sense of confirmation, when it came to placing this baby. They called the neighboring office in Spokane, where the social worker there reviewed with them his list of eligible families, a list we weren't on. The conference call ended with all involved feeling no inspiration.

As the Spokane social worker went back to put away his list, however, his eyes fell on our file. He told us later how a feeling had come over him that this was *our* baby, and that he should call Seattle back. He did, and they responded positively but suggested that it would be prudent and appropriate, since it was a Friday, to take the weekend to ponder and pray. On Monday, it was unanimously felt that this baby did indeed belong to us. On Tuesday, in grateful disbelief, Sharon and I set out for Spokane to add a fourth pea to our pod.

The unusual events leading to Garrett's placement in our home inspired me throughout his life. In hindsight, I believe more was at work than just a social worker happening to glance upon our file. It seems to me that Providence knew this child was bringing very special challenges to Earth and that he would need a very special mother—a mother just like Sharon—to help him go as far as he could go.

For me, Garrett with his curly brown hair, big brown eyes, chubby cheeks, and ready smile was yet another case of love at first sight. His baby pictures looked similar to my own and, throughout his life, Garrett seemed to take pride in reporting to me whenever adults complimented him on how much he looked like his dad. Indeed, the similarity in physical features Brittany and Garrett shared with Sharon and me often surprised strangers when they discovered our family ties were of love and not of blood.

After signing all the necessary legal documents, Garrett needed his diaper changed. When the cool air of the air-conditioned room hit his wet, warm, bare bottom, he went off like a fountain, proving to us that he was all there, and all ours. It would be nice to have another boy in the house.

During the car ride home to Pendleton, we counted our many blessings. Our family, it seemed, was now complete. We wondered how Brittany would respond to a new baby brother. Until now she'd been the center of our family universe. Would she be willing to share the attention of her mom and dad? The answer came when we picked Brittany up from our baby-sitter. I knelt down and held Garrett out to her and announced, "Brittany, this baby is your new brother!"

She took one look at Garrett and exclaimed, "I don't like it! I don't want it!" Then she punched him in the nose.

Gradually, and to our great relief, curiosity over this new creature in our house got the best of her and she was demanding her turn at holding and cuddling "our little bear cub."

A few weeks later, our social worker called. Garrett's

birth-mother was having a very difficult time. She was unusually and profoundly depressed, and concerned whether we liked our baby. The social worker asked Sharon to write to her and assure her that the child was safe and secure, healthy and happy, and loved, even treasured. This was done and delivered through the agency in order to keep all our identities confidential and we soon received a reassuring reply that she was doing better, that she was relieved to hear firsthand of the baby's welfare, and that all was well.

At the time, I felt it must be entirely normal for a birth-mother to feel anxiety in putting her child up for adoption, and postpartum depression among all new mothers is more common than many people think. But, looking back with Garrett's long struggle with depression in mind, I now wonder if this exchange of letters signaled something more—perhaps a serious predisposition to depression passed on to him genetically. The answer, I suspect, is that most people are a blend of nurture and nature and are left with sufficient capacity to freely make choices and experience consequences, good and bad. Not a day goes by that I don't feel thankful for the birth-mothers of our children, thankful that they chose to give them life.

FOUR

In most respects, Garrett's babyhood was entirely normal and healthy. But he was slow to roll over, slower still to walk, and his speech was somewhat impaired, though his mistakes were adorable and endearing: "bawee" for *very,* "yike" for *like,* "vee vee" for *TV,* "mazageen" for *magazine,* and "Helm Fodder" for *Heavenly Father.* When he was three, we enrolled him at the Presbyterian preschool in Pendleton, where they asked to test him for speech difficulties. He tested on the low end of normal, so we were not much worried. Time, we were sure, would take care of his speaking skills and, thankfully, that turned out to be the case.

It did worry me that before falling asleep at night, Garrett would often thump his head on his pillow, over and over again, sometimes violently. When we asked Garrett's pediatrician about this, he assured us it was nothing to worry about— some children did it to stimulate sleep. We were glad to learn that it was a normal behavior, but I still found the image of my son trying to hurt himself disturbing.

One worry we did not have about Garrett was his appetite. He weighed in at ten pounds at birth and it was all up from there. He came with a sweet tooth, so he fit right in to the Smith family. Each day that Sharon picked him up from preschool, he would greet her with a smile and a question: "Momma, do you want to go out and get some lunch?" They would, and despite Sharon's nutritional pleadings, Garrett would always want to order "those greasy potatoes" and chase them down with something sweet. Throughout family dinners he offered running commentaries over culinary delights, saying things like, "Ahh, good juice!" or "Good meat, Mom!" and "You're a good cooker, Mom!"

On one occasion, however, his tabletop exuberance created a calamity. I returned from work one evening, hungry and anxious to eat. Sharon was putting the finishing touches on yet another delicious family dinner while Garrett, then in his "terrible twos," sat in his chair, awaiting his food like a young grizzly. Not yet fully familiar with Newton's Law of Gravity, Garrett rocked on the back two legs of his chair, and as we all sat down, he finally lost his balance. Falling backward, he grabbed the tablecloth, pulling the entire meal onto the floor after him. What a commotion! What a mess! Garrett staggered up, covered in gravy and the remnants of a meal, simpering, "I'm bawee, bawee sowwy, Daddy." We scrubbed Garrett and the floor, went out to a local restaurant, and have laughed about Garrett's "culinary catastrophe" ever since.

The years of Garrett's infancy were also the last years of my father's life. Dad often came up from Arizona to teach me the tricks of the trade. He was without question one of America's foremost authorities in food processing, and I was very fortunate to learn from him, to draw on his extensive experience and his inexhaustible network of industry contacts. Toward the end, he came with me to the Campbell Soup Company to tie down our largest sale—20 million pounds of frozen vegetables. He was quiet during the negotiations, as prices, quality, and quantity were hammered out, and I wondered why. Afterward, he pulled me aside. "Son, that was well done! You don't need me anymore. You've got the gift. You can sell ice to Eskimos and coals to Newcastle." It was a proud moment.

But I was prouder still of the close relationship he had developed with Garrett. He loved to play hide-and-seek with his grandson and showered both Garrett and Brittany with candy, gifts, coins, bear hugs, and kisses. He and Garrett were inseparable in life, and they now lie next to one another at the Pioneer Cemetery in Weston, Oregon.

FIVE

Throughout the 1980s, I focused on improving the fortunes of Smith Frozen Foods, doing whatever was necessary to increase sales and expand production. As my father had realized that day at Campbell Soup, my talents were best suited to sales, so I spent a great deal of time traveling to San Francisco, Chicago, New York, Tokyo, Hong Kong, and wherever else I could find a buyer and make a sale. The thousands of sales calls I've made blur in my mind, but what I remember most was wanting to get home and feeling thankful when I did, sometimes after heroic measures to persevere through inclement weather or canceled and overbooked flights. Home is always where my heart is, even when my body is somewhere else. And throughout, I always took solace and too much license in knowing that Brittany and Garrett had the best care in the world with Sharon.

Whenever I arrived home, whether it was from a late night at the plant just a few miles away, or from a sales call on the other side of the world, I knew I would be greeted by a scene that sometimes seemed straight out of a Norman Rockwell painting. Our home was filled with the warmth and busyness that only a loving mother and lively children can create.

Once, when Garrett was five years old, I returned home from a long trip just in time to take him on a church-sponsored camping trip—his first fathers-and-sons outing. While Garrett ran about with his friends, I set up our tent, rolled out the sleeping bags, and built a campfire. I cooked us a passable meal, nothing great but something perfectly edible, and Garrett wolfed it down. Then he went on the prowl. Apparently, to him

I'd only fixed the appetizers, and he proceeded to go from campfire to campfire, cadging hot dogs, marshmallows, and every manner of soda pop and candy offered by the other fathers and sons. After all, he *was* a young grizzly. The memory of him having fun, unleashed to run about with his buddies, making mischief and discovering the natural world, remains fondly fixed in my mind.

What happened next I don't remember quite as fondly. No dad likes to say no to his little boy when he's having so much fun, but what I didn't realize was that in all the fun, he was also making himself sick. As we entered our tent to get ready to go to sleep, he promptly threw up. Garrett felt better, but what a mess! It seemed that s'mores were everywhere, and we needed to sleep anywhere but there. We abandoned the tent, and Garrett helped as much as he could while I cleaned up the sleeping bags. At long last we crawled into them outside, under the blue vault of heaven. It was a gorgeous starry night in the Blue Mountains of eastern Oregon. The Milky Way seemed painted in the sky just for us and I pointed out various constellations to Garrett.

"Where's Heavenly Father live?" he asked.

"I don't know, Garrett," I said. "But I do believe He's up there."

Garrett made a small, satisfied sound and with that, sleep seemed to finally settle on him after all the excitement. It was quiet except for the crackling of the fire, the creaking and croaking of countless creatures, the sounds of nature at night. But then he rolled toward me.

"Daddy," he whispered.

"Yes, little buddy," I whispered back.

"I like sleeping out here with you and the bears."

I liked it, too.

There was always a natural spirituality to Garrett's character and a childlike quality to his faith. He was teachable and never rebellious. He seemed to know right from wrong instinctively. He was well behaved in school and never acted up in public. He didn't like "bad people" and was repelled by "mean people." In fact, his favorite television cartoons were those featuring superheroes. He delighted in their success in setting things right and doing good for others and proclaimed that one day he would like to be in the "bad-man-shooting business." His favorite childhood toys were Care Bears, Cabbage Patch Kids, and all manner of stuffed animals. Like most boys, however, as he grew older, his interests migrated to Hot Wheels, Legos, toy guns, and anything that went *boom.*

But Garrett never outgrew his natural tenderness or his unusual thoughtfulness. When he received money as a present from a relative, he wouldn't use it to buy himself a toy or treat. Instead, he'd invariably buy something for Brittany. He cried readily over the pain and suffering of others. Once, when I picked him up at Scout camp, I found him disconsolate over a chipmunk that some of the other Scouts had cornered and killed. Years later as a teenager he would enjoy shooting guns and going on hunting trips, but he was really there for the camaraderie, never the kill.

When Garrett was in kindergarten, I was given two tickets to a *Monday Night Football* game in Seattle, and I decided to bring him with me. As the plane descended into Seattle, his little face was pressed against the window, enthralled with the city below. "This is where I'm from, Daddy! Isn't it awesome?" he exclaimed. (From their earliest days, Sharon and I told our children in positive terms about their adoptions, where they were born and what we knew about their birth parents. We explained to them that adoption is natural and wonderful, and encouraged them, if ever they felt the need, to seek out their biological genealogies.)

When we landed in Seattle, I needed some cash for a cab and for the food and souvenirs I knew Garrett would like at the game, so I headed for an ATM. I inserted a credit card, punched in my PIN, and out came the cash. While we walked away and I stuffed the money in my wallet, Garrett began tugging hard on my shirtsleeve.

"Daddy, don't you want to try it again?" he asked. "We're getting rich here!"

Nobody could make me laugh like he could.

Garrett also enjoyed playing the occasional, harmless practical joke on his parents. Many times Sharon would be vacuuming, when, all of a sudden, the vacuum would stop. She'd turn around to see Garrett running away, laughing uproariously at pulling the plug. And if I happened to fall asleep on the couch, Garrett would invariably jump on top of me. I returned the favor many times.

Of course, along with all the fun we had with Garrett, there were times he needed correction, but those duties usually fell to

Sharon because of my absence or my preference for playing Santa Claus in the lives of my children. I'm a poor disciplinarian. But on one occasion I came home, tired and ill-tempered, to find that Garrett and some neighborhood boys had broken the windows of an abandoned shed next door, an act of juvenile vandalism that struck me as especially wanton for a five-year-old. I spanked Garrett hard and sent him to his room with instructions not to come out without my permission.

Within minutes, I felt terrible, positive that I'd overreacted. Immediately, I went to retrieve Garrett from the purgatory to which I had banished him. When I got there, I found his door open, my son sobbing in the shadows of the hallway. He held out his arms to me.

"Please forgive me, Daddy," he pleaded. "Please love me again!"

I gathered him in my arms. "Garrett, I promise to love you always and forever." I've never forgotten the lesson Garrett taught me that day about being a gentler father and a more forgiving person.

Garrett's capacity for caring and sharing was perhaps best shown in 1989 when we were given the unexpected opportunity to adopt a third child. Sharon and I received a phone call from Dr. Steven Lamb, a Pendleton physician, who told us of a young unwed mother he was treating. She wanted to put her unborn child up for adoption upon its birth. Would we be interested? And, if so, would we be willing to pay the hospital expenses?

It was another thunderbolt in our lives, arriving out of the clear blue sky. As our home and our hearts were fully expanded by now, and our experience in adoption had been entirely positive, Sharon and I discussed the potential ramifications for our family. We both felt good about it. The next day, Sharon talked to Brittany and Garrett about the possibility of our family growing larger by one.

Immediately afterward, Garrett, though only seven years old, called me on the phone at work. "Daddy, I'd really like a little brother!" he said. "Can we have this baby?"

"Well, Garrett, the baby might turn out to be a girl."

He paused for the shortest of beats. "Another sister would be okay, too. Please, Daddy, please. We need another baby!"

How could I argue with that? I assured him that his mother and I also wanted another baby, and we soon told Dr. Lamb of our interest. A few months later, we welcomed Morgan Spencer Smith to our family. He arrived with flaming red hair, and Garrett could not have been happier with his new baby brother.

SIX

As Sharon and I continued to do our best to juggle the responsibilities of family and a growing business, suddenly the demands on our time nearly doubled. I was appointed—or "called" in Mormon vernacular—to serve as the bishop of one of the Pendleton Wards. You don't campaign or even volunteer for this position in Latter-Day Saint laity. You are asked and you accept. In another denomination it would be the equivalent of a pastor, rabbi, or priest, but it comes without pay. A bishop's responsibility knows no clock or calendar; requires every imaginable skill in counseling, consoling, correcting, and encouraging; is never fully completed; and is sometimes exhausting but always satisfying and soul stretching. My duties now were not only to my family and my employees, to farmers and customers, but also to some 600 souls who counted on me for leadership and stewardship in all the ecclesiastical services and welfare programs of the Church.

Sharon, as always, was my perfect companion in shouldering this new burden. Her unofficial title was "Mother of the Ward." In this capacity she was tireless in visiting and helping the sick, the shut-ins, the lonely, the widowed, and the fatherless. It seemed that whenever I came home, the aroma of a meal Sharon was cooking to take to someone else in need greeted me at the door.

Unfortunately, I wasn't walking in our door nearly as much as I would have liked. As my duties at work and church increased, my time at home decreased, so it also fell to Sharon to take up the slack I was leaving in the rearing and nurturing of our children. It must also be said, though, that our family enjoyed many compensating blessings during this incredibly challenging time. We were still young, in good health, and with sufficient strength for hard work and long hours. Our business prospered in extra measure, and Smith Frozen Foods was soon providing an average of 10 to 15 percent of all U.S. frozen peas, corn, and diced carrots. Garrett had begun his school years with an abundance of good teachers and good friends. He was easy to like and he liked everyone back, always offering that infectious, enticing smile. Indeed, in many ways, these were our halcyon days.

Things began to change when Garrett was in third grade. For the first time his learning disabilities became apparent. Though his ability to do arithmetic was encouraging, his reading and writing skills seemed stuck in the rudiments. He struggled to place words in sequence and his ability to memorize deteriorated. Still, for the longest time, he didn't lose heart. Indeed, Sharon and I will always treasure a letter we received after Garrett's death from his sixth-grade reading teacher. In recalling Garrett's difficulties with reading, she wrote, "As an experienced veteran teacher, I have witnessed countless children who have suffered from learning obstacles. But I have encountered no one who tried harder than Garrett. It was heart breaking to watch someone who was so bright and articulate struggle so."

Seeing him struggle, we had Garrett tested by a psychologist with the Pendleton School District. We learned that our son had a very high IQ, but had an overlay of dyslexia. This combination of good gray matter without the hard wiring to utilize it would cause Garrett endless frustration in the years to come and would lead, eventually, to a catastrophic crippling of his self-esteem.

Maybe that's the hardest thing for me to understand, how he could have seen himself as anything less than wonderful. If only he could have seen himself through my eyes, seen what a treasure he was to us. Garrett was always getting his mother or me to read to him. He rarely went to bed without one of us sharing a bed-time storybook. He especially loved *Charlie and the Chocolate Factory, Charlotte's Web,* and The Boxcar Children mysteries. Garrett would listen intently to each story and seemed to live through the experiences of the characters. He especially loved happy endings. When the chapter was over and it was time to turn out the light, Garrett was always grateful. He'd say good-night with that big grin of his shining in the darkened room.

Though he wasn't a natural athlete, Garrett was great at recess. Because his dexterity and his hand–eye coordination were a beat slow, his reflexes tended to be defensive, but he could run fast in a straight line and his body was built with big bones and strong muscles. This meant that in Little League baseball he could never hit a curveball—in fact I can't remember him ever getting a hit, but I do remember him reaching base a lot when the pitchers hit *him*. When it came to Pop Warner football, and later in high school, Garrett made himself into a fine defensive lineman.

Rather than trophies and individual glory, sports for Garrett were about being part of a team and being there for his teammates. As a high school wrestler, Garrett made us cancel any number of vacations so that he could participate in holiday tournaments. He didn't want to let down his friends and his coach. We were glad to stay home and were very proud to see that Garrett was learning some of the best lessons that come from team sports: dedication, commitment, and loyalty.

Amid all the hustle and bustle of our lives, we often found rest and relaxation in family ski trips. For a time we owned a condominium in Park City, Utah, and retreated there as often as work and other duties allowed. I put all my children on skis at an early age. Garrett's first instructor asked him to "make your skis into a pie," a common way to get kids into the snow-plow position. Garrett responded, "No pie. Make cake!" On hearing that, I realized that putting him on skis at three years of age might be too early. We came back and tried again the next year and, while never much for moguls, Garrett became quite a downhill racer and snowboarder. For all the obstacles in front of him, Garrett seemed to be handling them with character and courage. We were *always* proud of him.

Given the hectic pace of the Smith family, the help of many baby-sitters was necessary. One of these sitters, Sarah, bears mentioning, for she became part of our family. Sarah and her brother Seth came to this country from Korea and had been adopted by a family in Pendleton. When we met her, she was twelve years old and spoke little English, but she was tenacious in learning and industrious in helping Sharon with the chil-dren. We hired her often, for Sarah was mature beyond her years and the children loved her dearly.

Unfortunately, her adopted family soon broke up in a difficult divorce. Sharon got a call from Sarah's school counselor with a startling question: Could Sarah come live with us? Sarah did not want to remain with her adoptive family and we did not want to see her move away or return to Korea. She loved us and we loved her, but clearly we had no right to keep Sarah without the permission of her legal adoptive parents. They granted that permission, and Sarah became a Smith, in love, though not in law. From the moment she moved into our home she was no longer our baby-sitter, she was, in our hearts, our daughter. We watched with pride as she became an honors student at Pendleton High School, a graduate of Brigham Young University, a church missionary in South Korea, and, eventually, a beautiful bride to Dr. Shawn Frehner, a Las Vegas, Nevada, veterinarian. Today their children, Ashley and Michael, call Sharon and me "Grandma" and "Grandpa."

SEVEN

My cousin, Morris Udall, once famously said, "The only cure for political ambition is embalming fluid." I was no different. Having realized my dream of running the family business, my other boyhood ambition—politics—began to bubble up again in my mind, especially after a few years in the world of business. Clearly, few politicians in Oregon had ever signed the front side of a paycheck. Time and again they made it clear to me that they loved employees but didn't like employers. Oregon was in the midst of the recession of the early 1990s and many Oregonians were growing tired of paying for progressive politics. A taxpayer revolt was on the horizon.

During this period Garrett, who must have been nine at the time, came into the kitchen and announced to Sharon that he was bored and didn't have anything to do.

"Dad's in the family room watching television," she said. "Why don't you go watch with him?"

"No," Garrett demurred. "Dad just likes to watch people arguing about stuff."

Time and again, I found a thousand reasons to talk myself out of doing more than just watching politicians argue, and making a run of my own for public office. Five of those reasons were named Sharon, Brittany, Garrett, Morgan, and Sarah. The many demands on my time had already shortchanged them. Besides, I told myself, no one with my profile, a rural businessman and a Mormon bishop to boot, could ever be elected to anything in left-leaning Oregon. I didn't yet fully understand how tolerant a place Oregon truly is, big-hearted and open-minded enough even for someone like me. Oregonians, I have learned, don't care how you pray or where you pray or even *if* you pray. They want to know if you have reasoned and reasonable judgment, sufficient private and public integrity, and an ability to stay within the broad common-sense center of American politics.

One night, in the spring of 1991, after dinner and dishes, I turned on the evening news and was drawn to a story about a Southern governor announcing his candidacy for President of the United States. I remember being somewhat amused—the guy didn't have a chance. President George H. W. Bush was riding high in the polls with approval ratings greater than 90 percent, and basking in the afterglow of the Gulf War. But I also was struck by the governor's age: He was in his forties. I was about to turn forty. He was running for President, and I was just sitting on the couch, thinking about running for, well, *something*. Even with this dose of guilt, I again pushed away the thought. "Someday," I told myself, "someday you'll stop thinking about it and do it." That Southern governor who I didn't think had much of a chance? It was Bill Clinton, of course.

Some six years later, I found myself aboard Air Force One with President Clinton, heading to Paris as the representative of the United States Senate to attend the signing of the Russia-NATO Accord. I was reading a book when I became aware that the T-shirt-and-Levi-clad President of the United States had sat down in the cabin chair facing mine. In his warm and wonderful way, Bill Clinton wanted me to feel welcome and to get acquainted. I enjoyed immensely our visit and shared with him how he had helped spur me to enter politics. He seemed pleased at first, but President Clinton is a man who wears his feelings on his face, and it was easy to detect some chagrin at having played any role in electing a Republican from Oregon.

* * *

In 1991, flying on Air Force One was something I could not have imagined when I received a phone call from a neighbor named Don Cook. He asked whether I would go to lunch with him and a group of prominent Pendleton Republicans. I agreed and met them, anxious to hear what they wanted. They told me they were on an errand for the Republican leader of the Oregon State Senate, and that they wanted to back me in the 1992 election for the State Senate seat that encompassed Pendleton.

The longtime Democrat incumbent who had held that seat had recently resigned to accept a new job in Portland, and he'd been replaced by an appointee who wasn't yet politically entrenched. The time was ripe, they thought, for a Republican to take the seat, and that I was that Republican. I reminded them of what I perceived as my own electoral liabilities, but they stuck to their guns. I didn't say no, but I did ask for time to think about it and to seek Sharon's counsel. They said they'd give me all the time I'd need and told me that a fellow named Dan Lavey, chief of staff to the Senate Republican leader, would soon be calling on me.

Sharon's first reaction was, "Look, honey, you've gone from being a lawyer to a pea picker. And now you want to be a politician. Why do you want to keep going down the ladder of social acceptability?" She said this in fun, but I was sure she was thinking that if I ran, I'd get it out of my system, and we could get on with our lives.

Next, I went to see my ecclesiastical leader, Duane Wood, who served as the Stake President. I told him what was being asked of me, and that I was interested, but that because of my belief in and commitment to the separation of church and state, I should not, could not, and would not run for public office while presiding as a church bishop. As I laid the case before him, I knew that bishops were normally released after five years and that I had been serving for more than four.

President Wood thought for a moment and then said, "Bishop, if you want to run, we'll release you. If you don't run, we'll fire you."

When Dan Lavey called on me I expected him to be at least my age and a grizzled veteran of many political battles. I was stunned when a twenty-five-year-old walked in. Any doubts I had about his savviness were allayed, however, soon into our conversation. This kid knew politics and elections. He was wise beyond his years and had much more than just contacts and a title. Strategy and tactics were intuitive to him. He was a talent and, after a decade and more in hardball politics, I've seldom found his equal. I told him I would run, while at the same time telling myself I was crazy. But I wanted to do this, wanted it badly. I knew ambition for peas, and I felt it again for politics.

I was released as Bishop on a Sunday, and on the next morning I announced my candidacy with Sharon and our kids at my side. I organized my run as if it were a campaign for Congress, rather than for the State Senate. If I was going to lose,

I didn't want to look back at a lot of regrets. I hired another gifted consultant, Chuck Adams, to do my media and I set about knocking on ten thousand doors, giving speeches, and debating my fine opponent, Scott Duff, all over Senate District 29. Sharon once again rose to the occasion and proved to be an incredibly effective and charming campaigner, even winning the hog calling contest at the Wallowa County Fair. All in all, it was a textbook campaign that ended in a landslide victory on Election Day 1992.

Mr. Smith was going to Salem, Oregon's state capital. I was as excited as a kid on Christmas morning. I was good at selling peas, and I wanted to be good at fashioning public policy for Oregon. But I worried and hoped that my avocation for politics would not be harmful to my children. They seemed to enjoy the excitement of our first campaign, but now came the sacrifice. Sharon and I decided to buy a small house in Salem—some 250 miles from Pendleton—and to move the family there for the six-month legislative session, set to begin in January 1993. That required the kids to enroll in public school in Salem. Brittany and Morgan took the move in stride, and although Garrett's grades remained good and he quickly made friends in his fifth-grade class, Sharon and I worried that he sometimes seemed detached, uninterested, and a bit down.

It wasn't long before my worries turned to sadness. One day Sharon called me at my legislative office and asked if I could pick Garrett up from school on my way home. I found him sitting on a curb by the school, his big smile gone. He seemed depressed.

"What's wrong, buddy?" I asked him.

"Dad, something's wrong with me. I listen to the teachers, then look around at the other kids, and I think I'm the only one who doesn't get it. It's hard, Dad."

Another time, while Sharon and I were driving to a political event with the boys, we were reviewing the sequence of the months of the year with Morgan, preparing him for an expected quiz at school. Morgan, who was five years old at the time, quickly and correctly repeated them back to us. Garrett had been trying to follow along until he finally said tearfully, "I can't keep them straight and I'm seven years older." His face was full of sorrow and self-loathing.

I don't know if these episodes were more devastating to me or to Garrett, but I couldn't stop thinking about them. I did a great deal of soul-searching and wondered if my pursuit and service in public office was hurting Garrett. Sharon assured me that we could handle Garrett's challenges. Thanks in no small part to her tutelage and her professional training as a teacher, Garrett continued to bring home respectable grades throughout his schooling. I was proud of his efforts and grateful that Sharon was capable of keeping him afloat. Nevertheless, I hurt for Garrett, and I worried that his struggle with reading, his phonetic spelling, and his nearly illegible handwriting would hold him back or, worse, make him the object of taunts and teasing by classmates. That didn't happen, fortunately. He suffered no social stigma because he had the ability to hide his limitations and emotional scars behind his smile and friendly demeanor. Indeed, his friendliness and thoughtfulness always won him legions of friends, both boys and girls. He kept his hurt in his heart and at home.

EIGHT

The Oregon State Senate is a thirty-member body. The chamber was located across the Capitol rotunda from the sixty-member House of Representatives. The Senate had been under Democrat control since 1957. At times, the Republican caucus had been so small it could have fit into a phone booth. Republican fortunes changed with the election of 1992, and when the 67th Session of the Oregon State Legislature convened on January 11, 1993, there were thirteen other Republicans and sixteen Democrats serving alongside me in the Senate.

Life in the State Senate was endlessly interesting and intriguing. I worked hard, listened a lot, spoke sparingly, read voraciously, learned the rules for lawmaking, thought about policy, moved bills, offered amendments, won appropriations for my district, and made many friends among Republicans and Democrats alike.

The 67th session proved to be the longest in Oregon history up to that point, not adjourning until August 5. As the session drew to a close, the Senate Republican leader announced his resignation from that position. By a combination of good luck, good timing, and good friends, a coalition of senior members and the freshmen of my class (first-term senators elected the same year) elected me as the new Republican leader. My primary responsibility in this position, and the expectation of my caucus colleagues, was to see that the 1994 elections would result in the first Republican majority in four decades. Anticipation was high and my determination was higher. I had learned, both in peas and politics, that preparation and perspiration led to success. I took on this opportunity as yet another full-time job.

Ever since throwing my hat into the political ring, I had relied more and more on a wonderful management team at Smith Frozen Foods: Kelly Brown, David Jensen, Morris Hansen, Gary Crowder, David Stoddard, and Kent Perkes, to name only a few. I remained involved, as best I could, but at a distance. My plant and my new political duties were at opposite ends of Oregon. But the staff ran the business well without me and they gave me the freedom to pursue politics at a higher level.

In June 1993, after the school year ended, Sharon and the children moved back to Pendleton and I went home as often as possible, though my bases of operation were now in Portland, Salem, Eugene, and other communities up and down Oregon's populous Willamette Valley. Again, I rationalized that success in anything required sacrifice and I believed I had an aptitude for and a future in government. I certainly had a passion for politics. Besides, I told myself, I had Sharon's wholehearted support, and the children benefited from her remarkable gifts.

Election Day 1994 will be remembered as bringing about one of the biggest coast-to-coast Republican victories in American history, a wave that reached even the Oregon State Senate. Good candidates and a strong campaign plan, combined with the Republican tide, gave us a resounding 19-11 Senate majority.

When the 68th session of the Oregon State Legislature convened in January 1995, my colleagues elected me as president of the State Senate, the first Republican to hold that position in forty years. I was sworn in by the chief justice of the Oregon Supreme Court with my family—including my mother and my brother Milan Jr.—surrounding me. It was a day of great joy, tempered only by the fact that my father, who had passed away in 1987, would have enjoyed the occasion more than anyone else.

My new responsibilities as Senate president meant I'd be spending even less time at home (if that were possible), and Sharon and I redoubled our efforts to make family time meaningful. We took more family trips. Garrett seemed especially to enjoy family vacations and, throughout his life, he would often regale us with his memories of them. At school, Garrett soldiered on, doing his best on homework, term papers, and tests. We were proud of each other, father and son, but when I think about it now, I fear that, between his struggles in school and what he saw me achieving in state government, an emotional gulf was opening in Garrett's mind. While my political star was on the rise, his self-esteem was in decline. My public prominence too often placed him on the stage and in the spotlight as

well, when he preferred to hide behind the curtain, camou-
flaging the limitations he felt about himself.

The positive reviews I received for leading the Senate,
through what many agreed was one of the most productive legislative sessions in recent memory, fueled speculation among
pundits that I would one day be a candidate for higher office,
most likely the United States Senate. I confess I was thinking
the same thing, but at the time Oregon's two Senate seats were
occupied by a pair of five-term Republicans, Mark Hatfield and
Bob Packwood. Senator Hatfield was chairman of the Appropriations Committee, and Senator Packwood was chairman of
the Finance Committee. Together, they made Oregon the most
powerful state on Capitol Hill.

But the situation changed quickly in the summer and fall
of 1995, when Senator Packwood was caught up in a sexual
harassment scandal that eventually led to his resignation.
Oregon law required a special election, with a two-month
primary contest, followed by a two-month general election
campaign.

The United States Senate has been a fulcrum in our nation's
history. It has been the place where so many of our nation's best

citizens—as well as a few of our worst—have come to determine America's, and the world's, direction. Beginning in my boyhood, it represented to me an ideal, the ultimate place to do good and to produce the best for America. I wanted to go there, if I could, and do everything I could to achieve the lofty goals found in the Preamble to our Constitution: "to insure domestic Tranquility, provide for the common defence, promote the general Welfare, and secure the Blessings of Liberty to ourselves and our Posterity. . . ."

With idealistic thoughts in my head and a fire burning in my heart, I raised the question of running for the U.S. Senate with the children over Sunday dinner. Sharon had already given me her support, but she was concerned for the kids. Moving temporarily across the state was one thing, but moving for an indefinite period across the country, away from the life we loved in Pendleton, was quite another.

Brittany was immediately on board; she'd come to enjoy the spotlight of public life. Morgan was indifferent; frankly, he was still too young to understand the difference. Garrett, however, seemed stunned and fearful. Though quiet at first, he then started to cry, saying simply, "Dad, I'd rather you run for coach."

I was devastated by Garrett's answer and I am haunted by it still. After he stopped crying, Garrett and I talked through the matter for some time. I told him how badly I wanted to run, and that, if I ran, I would do all I could to minimize the impact on him. I also shared my own experiences of growing up in the nation's capital, and I described the wonderful opportunities and experiences that awaited him there. His mood brightened as we talked, and finally he gave me his permission to run.

After winning the Republican nomination, I faced off against the Democratic nominee, eight-term Congressman Ron Wyden of Portland. Our race will be remembered as short, brutish, and nasty. I knew politics wasn't beanbag. State legislative races can be hard-hitting, but I never imagined how much national hardball could hurt, especially a special election for the United States Senate. The lights are on and the heat is intense. While each of us bore responsibility for our own campaigns, no sooner had the race begun when the national parties, the White House, and outside interest groups came in and took it over. They defined our candidacies in extremist terms, turning it into a national referendum on the "Republican Revolution" led by Newt Gingrich (a man I had never met), and a test of President

Clinton's ability to get off the mat after the drubbing the Democrats took in the mid-term 1994 elections. It was ugly, mean, defamatory, even dehumanizing. I hated it. Two months seemed an eternity and I lost thirty pounds through work and worry. We debated often and we campaigned constantly and Oregonians couldn't wait for it to end. Neither could we.

I did go home each Saturday night to spend Sunday with the family, resting up and attending church. One Saturday night, I came home completely exhausted, fell into a comfortable chair, and immediately fell to sleep. I awoke when little Morgan tapped me on the wrist and asked the startling question, "Daddy, can I have your watch when you're dead?"

I didn't die, but I did lose, by 1 percent, in one of the closest Senate elections in Oregon's history. I had run as hard as I could, coming from 40 points behind in the beginning, and eventually winning thirty of Oregon's thirty-six counties. I lost the election by getting swamped by overwhelming numbers in Multnomah County—Oregon's most populous county—and the home of Ron Wyden's congressional seat. After the results came in, I made a congratulatory phone call to Ron and a concession speech to my supporters. I told them that in our great democracy we always get to have our say, but that we don't always get to win. We'd had our say and they had my eternal gratitude. Sharon, the children, my mother, and many siblings were at my side that night to bear me up. I appreciated their presence and support. But what to do next? I had never lost anything important in my life. A test of my heart lay before me.

The first call I received on the morning after the election, at approximately six A.M., was from Senator Hatfield. He congratulated me on running a good race and told me he wanted to help me run a better one. He reminded me that his fifth term was ending at the end of the year, and that he had announced a few months earlier that he would not be running for a sixth (though he surely could have won it). He urged me to keep right on running. He told me many other encouraging things and shared with me the fascinating pedigree of his Senate seat. It had first been held by Edward Baker, Abraham Lincoln's friend and former law partner, as well as by Charles McNary, a former Senate Republican leader.

"You see," he told me, "the seat is a historically Republican one, and I believe you can keep it—that way if you can find the physical stamina and emotional strength to immediately begin running again."

I thanked the senator for his thoughtfulness and encouragement and then drove to Salem to preside over a brief special session of the State Senate. Colleagues surrounded me with support and condolences, and when I finally drove back to Pendleton, I was an emotional mess.

I was truly torn. Part of me wanted to keep up the fight and to make the difference I felt I could make as a United States senator. Another part of me said I'd done enough, done all that I could or should in public service. I was down, even depressed, and didn't want to leave my family again to go back into the fire of another campaign. But encouragements kept pouring in from around the state and country, and something down deep inside told me that I had to get up and try again. As one supporter put it: "Gordon, the only way to take the pain out of losing is to go out and win!"

Sharon, too, had seen the light in my eyes dim, my normal enthusiasm ebb, and encouraged me to run one more time because she wanted her old husband back again. Each of the children, in their own ways—Garrett, too—said, "Get going, Daddy!"

So on a beautiful spring morning in 1996, in Portland's gorgeous Rose Garden, with Mt. Hood glistening in the distance, before a throng of press, supporters, and again with my family at my side, I announced that I was in the race for Senator Hatfield's seat. Garrett was always a bit mystified by these noisy events, but he was always a good sport about them, too. In running, I became the first person in United States history to run for both his state's U.S. Senate seats in a single calendar year. (I've often joked that I'm also the first person in U.S. history stupid enough to try it.)

My first steps on the campaign trail were halting. My heart was still healing and I lacked the essential hope that I could win. But this time I hired a general consultant named Kieran Mahoney from New York, who'd helped elect Republicans in places far more challenging than Oregon. He not only showed me that I could win, he convinced me that I would. Kieran wrote the campaign plan and we followed it, through all the twists and turns that come with any campaign. As each day went by, I got stronger emotionally and electorally. I had no serious opposition in the May primary and cruised to an easy victory. My general-election opponent was a high-tech multimillionaire right out of central casting named Tom Brugerre. He was handsome, smart, well-spoken, had a lovely family, and all the money he needed to run a strong race. And Tom did run a good campaign, but this time we ran a near-perfect one. The weekend before election day, my Oregon pollster, Bob Moore, told me that I was up by eight percentage points, but that, given the likely Clinton-Gore re-election landslide in Oregon, I would probably surrender half of that lead on Election Day. That's exactly what happened. This time, Mr. Smith *was* going to Washington!

The first thing I did after my victory was assured was to call Ron Wyden. While my last call to him had been to concede, this call was to invite him to breakfast the next morning. Since we were now to be colleagues, for the good of Oregon we had to put the bitterness of the previous campaign behind us. He agreed wholeheartedly, and before the orange juice was poured, we had taken the first steps toward what has become a true friendship. We have served together for nearly a decade now, and we regularly hold joint town hall meetings, publish a bipartisan agenda, and when Congress is in session, we get together at least once a week for lunch to compare notes, exchange ideas, and decide what we can do from across the aisle to advance

Oregon's interests. In doing so, I hope we have set an example for our colleagues: that elected officials should be Americans first and partisans second, and that much can be accomplished when Republicans and Democrats work to find agreement rather than just always finding fault.

NINE

In December 1996, Sharon and I traveled to Washington, D.C., for Senate orientation meetings, and to decide where and how to relocate our family. We agreed that my life's pursuits should not disrupt the children in the middle of another school year, so therefore Sharon and the kids would remain in Pendleton until the school year was complete, and then join me full time in Washington the following September. At the time, my mother was living in a high-rise condominium in suburban Chevy Chase, Maryland. Several years after my father's death, Mother had met and married a wonderful man named Jose Gil. I accepted their gracious offer to use their extra bedroom until the family could join me.

While I knew I would greatly miss Sharon and the kids during those first eight months of my Senate term, I also knew that as a freshman senator, I would be returning home to Oregon as often as possible to see them and to keep in touch with my constituents. I would also come to treasure the additional time I had with my mother, who would pass away in 2001. What wisdom she had. What a woman she was. I always knew that she loved me, and was proud of me, but she also continually reminded me to give Sharon more help, and to get home more often to spend time with the children, especially Garrett. Senate business and travel, as important as they were, she argued, were much less important than family.

"I'll do better," I'd tell her. "I've always been faithful to Sharon, and the kids know I love them."

Then she'd give me that eagle-eye look I remember from church and say, "You love what you serve and serve what you love."

TOP: My parents, Milan and
Jessica, and their brood of ten
children (I am on the far left).

RIGHT:
Sharon's parents, "Lanky" and
Vivian Lankford.

June 6, 1975—the happiest day of my life. Sharon and I are married at the LDS temple in
Chevy Chase, Maryland.

My father, Milan Smith,
had a special relationship with Garrett,
showering him with candy,
gifts, coins, bear hugs,
and kisses.

Garrett, age four,
in his first preschool photo.

The Pendleton Round Up—one of America's largest rodeos—was always a special occasion. Garrett, in his cowboy finest, stands next to Chris Leonard, who was a loyal friend throughout Garrett's life.

Garrett's seventh grade photo. Although his dyslexia made school a challenge, his perseverance combined with Sharon's assistance allowed him to bring home good grades.

TOP: Given my busy schedule, family vacations—such as this journey to Hawaii—were always a priority. BOTTOM: Garrett and Brittany after the opening of her high school play. Garrett was an incredibly supportive and loving brother.

TOP: Our dogs, Ollie and Oreo, provided Garrett with an endless supply of smiles and laughter. BOTTOM: June 2000. No one worked harder to earn a high school diploma than did Garrett.

Top: Garrett with his
good friends Ben and
Ethan Brown in July
2000, three months
before his departure for
his mission in England.

RIGHT: Garrett and a
very proud dad at
Reagan National Airport
in Washington, D.C.,
as he departs for his
mission.

May 2002.

When I asked her later if she felt I should seek a second term, she answered in her honest and practical Udall way, "Well, two terms won't look any better on your tombstone, and family is forever."

And yet, she was also always urging me to climb on, to be better, to achieve greatly, but to never forget balance. When I was young and didn't hop right out of bed in the morning, Mother used to call down to my room, "Better get up, Gordy, or you won't amount to a hill of beans!" Once, during my time living with her and Jose, I slept through the alarm clock after a particularly long night of work in the Senate. As I slowly roused, I heard a knock on my door, and my mother's voice calling out once again, "Better get up, son, or you won't amount to a hill of beans!" Mothers! Thank heaven for them.

There's an old Senate saw that new senators spend their first year wondering "How did I get here?" and the rest of their years looking at their colleagues wondering, "How did *they* get here?" In my case, I wondered about the former, but not the latter, because I found my colleagues—Republicans and Democrats alike—in almost every instance to be wonderful men and women. They are competent, competitive, and, yes, occasionally combative, but they are, with a few exceptions, honorable and honest, modern-day patriots with strong views about how to make America better, to keep her fair and free and safe. Every day I feel it a privilege and a pleasure to go to work with such people, even while realizing that half of them are trying to get me fired. And in the midst of the war of words in Washington, it is sometimes forgotten just how fortunate we are as a nation that our weapons are just words, our contests are over ideas, that our progress is still the province of "we the people." After a decade in the Senate, whenever I see that gleaming Capitol dome, I still feel a tingle in my spine.

During those first months in the Senate, I immersed myself in all aspects of my work and soon found that the fundamentals of lawmaking and success were not all that different between the state capital in Salem, Oregon, and the nation's capital in Washington. The budgets had more zeros on them and the federal issues were most interesting to me. As much as I loved my work, I also loved getting back to Oregon and the family nearly every weekend.

TEN

G arrett used to tell us that there were three things he really wanted to accomplish. He wanted to become an Eagle Scout. He wanted to graduate from high school. He wanted to serve a church mission. Three very worthy goals and I never thought more of this except to wholeheartedly encourage him. Only occasionally did he mention marriage and family. I chalked this up to his natural shyness around girls and, to be honest, when most boys talk about the future, they list the mountains they'll climb and oceans they'll sail and assume all the rest.

The first goal he accomplished one weekend early in my Senate years, when we all attended his Eagle Scout Court of Honor. Eagle Scout rank is the highest advancement in scouting. A Boy Scout must fulfill substantial requirements in the areas of leadership, service, and outdoor skills. Earning an Eagle badge is a very difficult thing for a boy to do; only 4 percent of Scouts reach that level. But *he* had, and I couldn't have been more proud of him. In his acceptance remarks, Garrett gave special tribute and thanks to his mother and to his scoutmaster, Kent Perkes. He didn't mention me. I can't say that didn't hurt a little, but it was honest of him. I hadn't been there enough. But Kent Perkes, who was also my brother-in-law, former New Zealand mission companion, and lifelong friend, deserved Garrett's commendation. He'd stepped in when I couldn't be there and made his nephew his special charge. He was a godsend to Garrett's scouting experience. Every Eagle Scout's mother also gets a badge and no mother ever did more to earn hers than Sharon.

It was around this time, after helping Garrett with home-work and preparing herself for bed, Sharon heard Garrett sob-bing in his room. She rushed to him and asked, "What's the matter, Garrett?"

"Mom, I just realized that I'll never be able to get married."

"But why?"

"I'll never be smart enough to support a family."

Sharon did her best to comfort him and assure him that he was smart enough, that he'd get married, that there were many ways he'd be able to support a family. I wasn't home that night, but when I was with him next I gave him the same reassurances. His mood brightened and we were soon joking and laughing with each other. I thought Sharon and I had fought back the fog he was feeling. But all we'd done, really, was wish it away. I realize now that Garrett's self-doubts were beginning to cloud his mind and darken not only his sense of the future but also his ability to see it rationally. Sharon would later recall it as "one of those instances that at the time meant one thing and now means another." The fact was, we'd never thought he *wouldn't* get mar-ried and have a family. He was fifteen, with his whole life ahead of him. For all of his challenges, Garrett had the intelligence, character, and drive to achieve not only his three small goals, but love and fatherhood and many other kinds of personal success. But now he was starting to see a different, and darker, world than the one that we saw.

By September 1997, we'd purchased a home in Bethesda, Maryland, and the family moved in, delighted to be together full time again. Sharon and I thought at the time to let our children try private school so we enrolled them at the Bullis School in Potomac, Maryland, an excellent school that was rigorous in academics and inclusive in athletics. Brittany and Morgan both adapted to it well, and we had hoped that the relatively low student-teacher ratio would help Garrett, now sixteen, in his classroom work. After a few months, however, it seemed that his difficulties were multiplying. The load of homework was substantially greater than he was used to in Pendleton, and the burden fell all the more on Sharon to keep him from becoming discouraged by the increased competition.

I rarely got home before eight P.M. each weeknight, so I worked Garrett through long-range assignments like term papers. I enjoyed doing these assignments with him. He would pick the topics and I helped him find the supporting research.

After we read the material together, he would tell me what he thought about it, and I would write it out for him as he might say it. As with all the schools Garrett attended, we had met with his teachers to discuss strategies to help him and we all agreed that this kind of intensive assistance was the only way he could complete assignments. It took time, but it was time well spent. It created bonds between us that he already shared in abundance with his mother and it led him to ask me a question about my work. One night he said he'd heard in his civics class that the government spent a lot of money on medical research. I told him that it was true and that I wholeheartedly supported it.

"Do you think they'll ever find a medicine that can help kids like me who have trouble learning?" he asked, adding, "That would be so incredible!"

I swallowed hard and promised him I'd support and promote anything that could make that happen. For once, my work in the Senate seemed to have a direct effect on his life, and his expression changed from pleading and longing to hopeful and happy.

Sharon and I often asked Garrett if he was happy at Bullis,

and he always cheerfully told us that he was. He did well in football and wrestling, and he made some of the best friendships of his life, especially with Jack "J. D." Driscoll. He even worked up the courage to go out on the occasional date and to take one of his classmates to the prom. As far as we knew, Garrett was coping adequately with the stresses and strains high school puts upon all kids, not just those with challenges.

We soon learned how exactly he was coping. In the spring of his junior year, the police called us to come and get Garrett, whom they were holding in a nearby park. They told us that some high school students were partying there. Beer had been liberally consumed. Garrett was one of many who were in no condition to drive.

Little was said as I drove Garrett home. I was probably still in shock from the phone call, but I understood that Garrett, who knew our family and church standards did not include the use of alcohol, was suffering plenty of remorse without my piling on more. The next morning, though, it was time to talk and that's when he dropped a bombshell on us. He told Sharon and me that the only way he could cope with all his anxiety was through drinking. He was afraid he was becoming

an alcoholic. An older brother of one of his friends was sup-
plying him with vodka and he was drinking each morning to
calm himself for the school day, then more at bedtime to help
him get to sleep. He had been self-medicating for some time,
going to elaborate lengths to hide it from us, stashing his
vodka bottles in the attic. Now he was crying out for help. He
still wanted to serve a church mission, but he knew his addiction would disqualify him.

We got him professional help through a youth drug and
alcohol program at a nearby hospital. The doctors there did not
diagnose depression or mental illness or make a connection
between drinking and depression, but they did warn us that
Garrett's chemistry made him highly vulnerable to addictive
behaviors. Sharon and I realized that we would have to watch
him like hawks, and help him stay away from situations that
might lead him to slip back. The biggest of those "situations,"
we concluded, was Washington itself. Life there clearly wasn't
working for Garrett. Seeing that, we decided that moving the
family back to Pendleton for his senior year would take a lot of
pressure off him. By now Brittany had entered BYU and
Morgan had shown that he could be happy in either place. We

were also given a supply of alcohol test strips, which Sharon regularly and randomly swabbed on Garrett's tongue. And not once, over the next year, did Garrett fail a test.

It was hard to watch the family leave. My hopes of giving them their own versions of my Washington boyhood were dashed. But I was also relieved that my own professional pursuits would no longer be an impediment to my children. While it was lonely to come home to an empty house each evening, and those weekend flights to and from Oregon were long and often frustrating, I was very content that Pendleton was a better place for Garrett.

In the months that followed, I felt even better about our decision. Garrett was noticeably more at ease in Pendleton, and he quickly reconnected with lots of his old friends. When school began in the fall, though, he didn't want to play on the football team or any other competitive sports. Instead, he was now into high-risk activities like cliff diving, bungee jumping, and auto racing. On the Saturdays when I came back, we would spend time together jet skiing, target shooting, tinkering with and talking about hot cars, maybe taking in a movie. After good-natured challenges to my manhood, he once coaxed me into performing a cliff dive, and during a family vacation to

New Zealand, goaded me into bungee jumping. Both times I accused of him of doing the bidding of the Democratic Party. It was laugh-out-loud fun.

Sharon and I sometimes attended various Pendleton High School sporting events, but Garrett joined us only on rare occasions. He didn't like crowds, he'd say. More and more, he sought solitude, playing with our two dogs, enjoying some off-road biking, or taking long drives over country roads. He asked for permission to move out of his bedroom, which was near Sharon's and mine, and to move into a vacant one in the basement. This made him feel more independent, but we certainly didn't leave him alone. It's easy to say now that we should have seen a pattern, the beginnings of a retreat into himself, but on their own, none of these events seemed out of the ordinary.

On school nights, most of which I spent in Washington, I'd always check in by phone, and offer encouragement as he and Sharon labored over homework. When they finished, he'd often compliment Sharon by saying, "You're an awesome mom!" Perhaps the best proof of how right Garrett was about his mom occurred when we were still in Washington. Because I was chairing the European Affairs Subcommittee on the Senate

Foreign Relations Committee, Sharon and I were attending a White House state dinner for the prime minister of Italy. State dinners are the preeminent social events in the nation's capital and this one was no exception. It was a sumptuous evening and the elite of the Italian-American community were gorgeously arrayed. Sharon had the good fortune of being seated at a table that included President Clinton, famed opera star Luciano Pavarotti, and movie icon Sophia Loren. A few tables away, I sought glimpses of Sharon through the candlelight illuminating the East Room, certain that she'd be entranced by the table conversation. But every time I looked over, Sharon was glancing at her watch. Between courses, I made my way over to her to ask if something was wrong.

"I'm worried about Garrett's homework," she said. "As soon as we can, we've got to get home."

I've never heard the priorities of a parent more eloquently expressed.

The day of Garrett's high school graduation, the day he completed his second goal in life, he seemed shy, even sheepish. I asked him why.

"They should be giving this diploma to Mom," he said. "She's the one that earned it."

I assured him that no one deserved it more than he did, and that we couldn't be prouder. And I meant it. GPAs and grades are one kind of measure, but in my eyes, Garrett was number one in his class. No one else, not even his counselors, coaches, and teachers, had seen the titanic struggle he'd gone through to get to the podium and hold that diploma. He'd hidden it behind that beautiful smile of his and a public persona somehow always personable and peaceful. One which we'd learn was just a mask.

ELEVEN

The summer following his graduation from high school Garrett pumped gas at a local service station in Pendleton and made plans to go on his mission. He took his physical exams, passed his ecclesiastical interviews, and checked a box on his application that indicated he had suffered from depression. When we asked him why he'd checked that box, he said that he didn't want to lie on his application, and that he felt depressed more and more. We asked if he would consider getting some professional help, and he assured us that he could handle his mood swings.

Over the years, I'd seen him go from glum to happy many times. In fact, Sharon and I did whatever we could to help him recover his good spirits, but we'd never thought of these shifts in his state of mind as abnormal. I was stunned by his self-diagnosis of depression. I didn't want to believe it and, like so many in our society, I didn't understand it. Sure, I thought, he'd had challenges, it was natural for him to be down about himself and about life at times; anyone in his shoes would feel the same way. Of course there was more to it than that and maybe if I'd had a personal reference point to what he was suffering I would have seen something other than a normal range of emotions. The only point in my life when I experienced real depression was after the loss of my first senatorial race, and that went away as soon as I went back to work.

A church leader called me to say that they were inclined to send Garrett on his mission but had some concerns about the fact that he'd checked the depression box. I told him of Garrett's challenges, but, not knowing any better, I played down the depression. Maybe I thought that somehow, if he got out into the world and involved in the work of making his own life, he'd simply stop feeling that way. I realize now, and too late, that Garrett's mental health, the hard wiring within his brain, made my diagnosis meaningless. To say to someone with manic depression or bipolar disorder, "Come on, buck up. Get to work!" is the equivalent of demanding a diabetic to make insulin. If you've never been swallowed by that infinite bleakness and hopelessness that accompanies manic depression, it's almost impossible to imagine.

Garrett soon received a letter informing him that his mission call would be to Manchester, England. Garrett was thrilled and relieved that it was to an English-speaking nation. He used to tell me he couldn't serve his mission in a country where he would have to learn a new language, because he still hadn't learned how to speak English!

We hit the stores to get him clothed and clad in missionary suits, shirts, shoes, ties, as well as raincoats and overcoats for the soggy English climate. We had a great time, though he felt

I was picking out entirely too many ties. I told him to take them anyway—they'd be his only fashion variable, given that missionaries are required to wear a plain dark suit and white shirt at all times. He did take them and he thanked me later, when he wrote from England asking me to send him some more. I later learned he had given most of them to missionaries who'd come to Manchester from eastern Europe. Garrett's heart was big and generous, and he was always giving away his material possessions to others whom he felt needed them more.

When Garrett left for England his biggest worry was whether he could learn the lessons and memorize the scriptures necessary to teach any who would listen. I told him not to be frustrated by that but to learn the concepts, and his companion missionaries would always be there to help when needed. I told him story after story from my own New Zealand mission. But mostly I told him to be good, to obey the mission rules, and to work as hard as he could. If he did that, I promised, he'd enjoy the greatest adventure in his life, and he would find happiness like he had never known before. With that in mind, and without a tear, he gave Sharon and me a big bear hug, boarded the plane, and soared into the sky. As I watched his plane take off, I was the one in tears.

TWELVE

T wo years of missionary service is an experience in the life of a young Mormon like no other. It is rigorous, regimented, refining, and revealing. There's little time for leisure, rejection by others is commonplace, exhaustion is often the result, and exposure to the best and worst of humanity is inevitable. But success and satisfaction are found in abundance and measured in the many good souls you meet and by the difference you are able to make in their lives. It is a time for service and sacrifice. Missionaries leave for their assignments as boys and girls. They return home as men and women.

Garrett was a good worker, and I knew he had the stamina for the job, but I worried whether the dark, dank British winters and the inevitable disappointments he would be faced with would cloud his mind. On the other hand, I knew that the lessons he would learn, the friendships he would make, and the companionships he would share would be a source of joy for him. And they were.

Each week Sharon dutifully sent him some small gifts, homemade treats, and a tape recording full of words of encouragement from the two of us. We shared experiences and expressed the pride we felt in him. Most weeks he sent back a tape of his own and we could sense tremendous growth and maturity emerging in him. When my mother suddenly passed away midway into Garrett's mission, he was not able to return for the funeral because mission requirements prohibited it. Instead, he recorded and sent to me the most thoughtful message of comfort and support. The boy Garrett was before he went to England could not have said and done what he did at that sad family moment. Our son was becoming a man, and our buttons were bursting in pride and hope for him.

While Garrett was away we prayed for him daily and thought of him constantly. With each passing day my duties and demands in the Senate were increasing, and I found satisfaction and success in fighting for Oregon's concerns in energy, health care, natural resources, high technology, and transportation, and in representing America's interests abroad. Because of my assignment to the Senate Foreign Relations Committee, my comments, as well as an occasional photograph, were often printed in the British press. These would invariably be brought to Garrett's attention. He seemed proud of me and he enjoyed the reflected celebrity status conferred upon him. Finally, I hoped, my public service was an advantage, not a hindrance, to my son.

Some months into his mission, I accepted an invitation to speak in London and Liverpool. Sharon traveled with me and, because Liverpool is not far from where Garrett was working, we were given permission to take him and his companion out for a meal. (Mission rules usually prohibit visits from parents or family members for the duration of a mission.) What we found was a young man without a crease in his trousers or a wrinkle in his soul. He confessed that he occasionally felt depressed, but that he was treasuring his experiences. He loved the English people, appreciated his mission companions, and found satisfaction in his work. Words cannot express how thrilled and relieved Sharon and I were. At last, Garrett was seeing and appreciating the good in himself and the daily wonders of life.

Shortly after we returned home, the unimaginable happened: September 11, 2001. On that beautiful fall morning, four planes flown by terrorists transformed our television screens into ugly scenes of murder and mayhem. Having never served in the military, I had not personally seen the face of battle, but I saw its remnants nine days after the terrorist attack when I went with Hillary Clinton and Rudy Giuliani to Ground Zero. Strewn amidst the mountains of rubble were the remains of my countrymen. The scene, the stench, the horror I saw, no sentence of mine can adequately describe. Deeply shaken, I returned that evening to a Capitol building that now resembled an armed camp to hear President George W. Bush's stirring speech of resolution and determination.

In the audience that evening was a man who momentarily

caused me to think of Garrett: Britain's great prime minister and America's stalwart friend, Tony Blair. We had earlier received word that Garrett was well and we had assured him that we were, too. In seeing the prime minister, who was seated next to Laura Bush, I also knew instinctively that Garrett was in a great place, among the stouthearted souls of Great Britain.

Two years fly by on wings of lightning when one is working hard at a worthy endeavor, and, before we knew it, Garrett was coming home. He was due to arrive two weeks after the celebration that annually turned my hometown of Pendleton into the rodeo capital of the world—the Pendleton Round-Up. Attendance at the Round-Up was a family tradition, and the 2002 celebration was to be even more special as Brittany was to reign over it as queen. I suggested to Garrett that we request a two-week early release in order for him to see his sister's big moment as rodeo royalty. He responded, "No, Dad, that's Brittany's day and I'm needed here. I want to finish the full two years." As much as Sharon and I would have loved to have had Garrett with us for this event, we were very proud of him for reminding us of the importance of fulfilling one's commitment and choosing duty before play.

When Garrett disembarked at Washington's Dulles International Airport, his face shone with the satisfaction that comes from completing a difficult job and doing it well. The mission president who oversaw Garrett's work in England confirmed this to us, saying Garrett had conducted himself with determination, shy dignity, and self-deprecating humor. Occasionally Garrett would fall quiet and let his companions do most of the talking and teaching, but he went to work every day and was much loved by fellow missionaries and church members alike.

When we stopped for dinner on the way home from the airport, it was clear that Garrett hadn't lost his appetite. Over a plate of ribs, he told us that he wanted to enroll at Utah Valley State College and room with his lifelong friend, Ethan Brown, who was also returning from his mission. Sharon and I were very heartened by Garrett's excitement and optimism and by the fact that he was looking ahead and planning for the future. We hoped and prayed that his newfound confidence would last in the face of the stresses and strains schoolwork would once again bring down on him—especially without the support he would normally have at home.

Still, things were looking up. Before I returned to the stump during my 2002 reelection campaign, Garrett and I went on another shopping spree to buy a car for school and to replace his missionary suits, which were now all in tatters, with new clothing for college. While we were shopping, I mentioned that I wanted to get his mother a ring to mark our upcoming thirtieth wedding anniversary and asked him to help me select just the right one. After finding one we both liked, he asked if I would return the favor and help him pick out a ring when he found the girl of his dreams. I told him that I would be honored to, and hoped that his college experience would include finding that girl. Garrett was to spend a few months in Pendleton before enrolling in college, and while I was campaigning across the state, he revisited the old haunts of his youth and reconnected with his friends. He even spent a few days cheerfully distributing and pounding placards into front lawns for my campaign.

That campaign ended with a landslide victory over Bill Bradbury, the Oregon secretary of state and a former colleague of mine in the State Senate. Bill is an affable and friendly fellow, but I won nevertheless with a 16 percent margin. As I

delivered my victory speech to hundreds of cheering supporters, with my family at my side, the world couldn't have
seemed much brighter. But it was soon to grow very dark.

Within weeks, Garrett's moods and behavior became suddenly and disturbingly erratic. On some days, he was optimistic
and excited about beginning school in Utah in January and
made plans with Ethan to find an apartment. On others, he
would take to his room and not come out for the rest of the day,
resisting encouragement even from his friends.

Sharon and I talked frankly with him about whether or not
some counseling would help. He assured us he was fine, and
then, just as if someone had hit a switch, his mood brightened,
his eyes twinkled again, and his big smile returned. We so desperately wanted him to be happy that we believed him, and
believed that he was just suffering an unusually difficult adjust-
ment period coming off the security and certainty of his mission. He would be better when he got into the routine of
college life, we hoped. He was, after all, twenty-one years old
and an adult. We told ourselves that his life with us and his mission experience had laid a firm foundation for his future. But
we didn't know the darkness of Garrett's demons and we had

forgotten, or dismissed as unthinkable, the warning once given us about his predisposition to addiction.

Sharon had seen to Garrett's enrollment at Utah Valley State College, where he'd applied for "special services" and qualified for extra help—tutors, notetakers, audio-visual aids, and extra time for tests. The classes he took were the general-education basics required of all freshmen. But now he had to take them alone, without the backstop of his mother. All we could do was pay for tuition and books, and hope and pray.

We called often to check in and to let him know how much we loved him. Garrett always assured us that everything was just fine. But it wasn't. Garrett attended his classes, attempted to study, and took his tests. But by February his depression had returned, his frustrations more ferocious than ever. Finally he called to say that maybe the time had come for him to try some antidepressant medication. This was quickly prescribed by a family physician and Garrett later told us that he thought the meds were helping. Socially, however, his life was going sideways. His flirtations with girls always ended in friendships, while his heart yearned for more. He was sleeping longer and more often than normal for a man his age. When friends invited him out, he usually took a pass. His decline grew even more precipitous when he turned again to alcohol. As before, he would drink privately and quietly, in the closets of his life.

His roommate, Ethan, began connecting the dots. He wanted to help Garrett but didn't know how. Though part of him wanted to tell us about what he saw, Ethan was his friend, not his enforcer or parent. But then one night he came home to find Garrett dangerously drunk and despondent. He had taken a third of a bottle of pain pills and washed them down with liquor. Ethan averted this first suicide attempt by staying up with Garrett, and walking him around the apartment for hours to keep him from passing out. Ethan finally got in touch with us, but like us, he was in denial. He told us he was worried about Garrett, but he didn't relate the details of the terrifying incident that had prompted his call.

Later, Ethan would tell us that he'd thought at the time that Garrett's drinking and depression had stemmed from "the pressure of school or girls and everything that happens when you move out on your own." Garrett claimed that the alcohol helped him to cope. "It helps me forget my problems," he'd said. "It numbs me, so I don't have to feel anything." Ethan urged Garrett to tell us that he was drinking again, and that he needed help, badly. In Ethan's opinion, part of Garrett's depression may have been because Garrett was hiding it from us. What neither of them probably realized is that alcohol operates as a depressant. It fuels depression and accelerates anyone already on that path to new, and even lower depths. "I never really imagined that he would actually take his life," Ethan mournfully admitted. Neither had we.

In April, Sharon and I traveled to Salt Lake City, and one evening we took Garrett and a date to dinner. He was all spruced up in his Sunday best, seemed happy, and it was clear that he was fond of the girl who was on his arm. But it was just as clear to me that his affection for her was unrequited. She liked him, sure, but as a friend, and I held my breath for him, hoping he wouldn't be hurt. But later, when he realized that she wanted only friendship, he was hurt, deeply so.

By semester's end, Garrett had scraped by, getting mostly Cs and a few Bs. He also had put on more weight and would only occasionally shave. He was sleeping too long into the day and sitting around silently long into the night. As Ethan remembered, "It wasn't just Garrett being quiet and keeping to himself. It wasn't just being under pressure. It wasn't normal." But it was enough of a red flag that, before leaving for a summer job, Ethan asked Garrett to surrender his hunting rifle to him. Garrett agreed.

Rather than coming home for the summer to work in the food processing plant, Garrett got a job in Utah. He wanted to stay in proximity to the girl he had grown so fond of, in the vain hope that her feelings for him would change and grow. He moved by himself into a new apartment complex near campus. He assured us all was well, but when Ethan again shared his concerns with us, and when a series of our voice messages to him were not returned, Sharon and I quickly decided it was time for a visit.

We flew to Utah and were alarmed by what we found. His weight had ballooned to over 200 pounds, his grooming was poor, and his countenance was dark. While he'd made some new friends in the apartment complex and at work, he confessed to us that his job was discouraging, that he was lonely in the now mostly deserted college town, and that the romance he had hoped for had never materialized. We noticed a scar on his upper arm from what looked like a knife wound, and when we asked about it, he shrugged it off as an injury he suffered in a mountain biking accident. We were anxious to believe him but learned later that it was indeed self-inflicted. A few months earlier, Garrett had agreed to see a psychologist and had assured us that he was still taking the medication that had been prescribed by a family physician. But I had my doubts, and Sharon and I were not about to leave after finding him in such a state, so I asked him what we could do to help him find happiness again.

He responded immediately, "Please take me back to England."

We leapt on the idea, seeing it as a chance to reconnect Garrett to a happy and fulfilling period of his life. Plus, we'd be able to spend concentrated, extended time with him. We quickly changed our Oregon plans for the Senate's August recess. I accepted invitations to participate in political conferences in Ireland and England and arranged for Garrett to meet us in London at the end of the conference. Before we departed for Britain, though, Brittany told us that she had discovered evidence that her brother was drinking again. Sharon responded to this better than I; she saw it more in medical terms. I, on the other hand, was irritated, even angry, and determined to find the right moment for rebuke. After all that we'd been through, I still couldn't comprehend the extent of his affliction and the danger he was in.

I rented a car in London and we told Garrett that we had a week to spend traveling wherever he wanted. Across England, Wales, and Scotland, mile after mile and town after town, Garrett's mood swings grew radical. Around his former British mission companions and church friends his reunions were truly joyful and he would be his wonderful self again. Climbing around castles and showing off his old areas of labor, he'd be as excited as a boy on Christmas morning. But driving away from these places, he'd tell us he didn't feel well and crawl into a near fetal position in the backseat, withdrawing from us emotionally and conversationally. That I couldn't reach and reason with him during these episodes filled me with fear and dread. He was, I recognized, more fragile than I ever realized and instinct cautioned care in any confrontation. So Sharon and I would drive on, hoping for an emotional resurgence as the beauty, pageantry, and history of the incomparable British landscape passed by our car windows.

Our last evening together was at Loch Lomond, Scotland,

and the time to talk was running out. Sharon began by reporting what Brittany had related about alcohol. What followed was harrowing and horrible. The dam of Garrett's emotions suddenly broke and he began sobbing uncontrollably. He screamed out that he wished his birth-mother had prevented his birth. He declared his life hopeless and valueless, his future futile. He was tired of being a burden to us and an embarrassment to himself and others. Pain and darkness so clouded his way each day, he shouted, that he dreaded the dawn, knowing it would only bring more anguish than the one before. He told us for the first time that he had experienced periods of dark depression since he was ten years old.

I was stunned into silence. I abandoned any plans for reproving him and tried to calculate the horror of what I was hearing. I felt hopeless as to how to help. As Sharon would later recall, "All of a sudden there was this steely look out of his eyes, the most frightening thing I have ever seen." He told us that the suffering of his mind was so painful that "I think I may take my life."

My son, I now fully realized, was mentally or emotionally ill—I didn't know which, or the difference. Nor did I know how to help. So I exhausted my abilities of expression and experience in youth counseling with words of comfort, encouragement, and love unfeigned. I assured him that he was loved by the Lord, treasured by family and friends, and precious to his parents. I promised him there was a good and happy place for him in this world and that I would do everything in my power, that I would exhaust every avenue, to help him find it. I begged him not to hurt himself, told him that we could not live without him, that we would get help for him, so healing and hope could return. Sharon and I were desperate, but he was beyond reach, beyond reason, beyond rationality.

"All I want," he said, "is to go to sleep without waking up."

We stayed with him all night long and, thankfully, with morning light, his mind and mood seemed to calm and brighten. On the flight back to the United States, we talked of possibilities, of future plans. I had long urged him to consider a military career or law enforcement or something that gave him structure and made him part of a team. But he talked about his fondness for cooking, expressed a desire to go to a culinary arts school, and wondered if I would help him someday get a restaurant or find a place for him in the quality-control department at the company. Whatever you want, I told him. He also asked if we could send him the family's English bulldog, Oliver, so he wouldn't be alone when he returned to Utah. He didn't want a roommate but felt Ollie would keep his spirits up. I told him that Ollie would be completely dependent upon him, so for the dog's sake, he would have to take good care of himself. He promised he would.

By the time we landed in Atlanta, Georgia, we'd made plans to meet again in a few weeks at the Pendleton Round-Up for a reunion with family and friends, and to talk further about his hopes and dreams for the future. In the meantime, while he wouldn't hear of hospitalization, he agreed to meet with an eminent psychiatrist in Utah. Garrett was to fly from Atlanta to Salt Lake City, and Sharon and I to Washington, D.C. As we said good-bye, he seemed his old self again. We hugged each other hard and I told him I loved him. Then he kissed Sharon on the lips—something he'd not done since he was a little boy. He told us he loved us and he walked away.

We never saw him alive again.

THIRTEEN

S haron and I would later piece together the last weeks of
Garrett's life from the memories of his friends. He regis-
tered for the fall semester at Utah Valley State College and
bought his books and supplies. He kept appointments with
his psychologist and the psychiatrist he had agreed to see and
was prescribed a new antidepressant and some potent sleeping
pills to restore normal sleeping patterns. The psychiatrist, who

saw him only once, detected nothing suicidal in anything Garrett said. If anything, he would later recall, Garrett was upbeat. But after only one visit, how could he have accurately diagnosed the depths of Garrett's downs or seen the heights of his highs? Once again, Garrett had shown his sunny side to a stranger and kept his disappointments and demons in the shadows. He desperately wanted others to see only his normality, not his difficulties, and I suspect his countenance was cheery. He had a new car. Ollie had arrived to keep him company, and he boasted to friends that the bulldog was a "babe magnet." Best of all, he believed that the girl of his affections had agreed to a Saturday night date.

But then, in quick succession, it all came unraveled. Someone backed into the side of his car in a parking lot. College buddies, who had planned to travel with Garrett to the Pendleton Round-Up, canceled. The landlord in Garrett's apartment complex told him that Oliver had to go, as dogs over twenty-five pounds were not allowed. (Ollie tipped the scales at sixty-five pounds.) And the longed-for Saturday night date? She called it off on Saturday morning.

In relating these events, we blame no one. Such events are

part and parcel of life's ups and downs, and for most people they amount to no more than frustration and disappointment. But, given Garrett's fragile mind and broken heart, they became a death sentence. So without revealing his intentions, he set about, in his own generous way, saying good-bye, just as he had been doing, we now realize, with us and his loved ones in England.

Earlier in the week he had helped a girl from Pendleton move her furniture into an apartment. Noticing that she did not have a television, he unplugged his and gave it to her. He also gave away his CDs and videos to a few friends and treated others to a meal at his favorite restaurant. He went to the local Red Cross and donated blood. He opened early the box of gifts Sharon had sent him for his twenty-second birthday. He purchased a bottle of Jack Daniels and replaced his friendly voice mail message with an ominous demand that no one should call anymore.

On Sunday he was seen playing with Oliver for the longest time on the lawn that fronted his apartment building. When they were done playing, Garrett ordered a pizza, made an enclosure in the kitchen for Ollie and included extra food and water. Then he wrote his suicide note, turned on soft music, and dimmed the lights.

My mind still struggles to imagine what he next did. Sometime in darkest night he swallowed all his sleeping pills with a large quantity of whiskey. Then, before he passed out, he knelt alone in his closet with a noose about his neck to make sure that, this time, he could "go to sleep without waking up."

It is hard for me to fathom how anguished and tormented a soul he had become, how hopeless and alone he felt in mind and spirit when, to all outward appearances, his psychological sufferings were so disproportionate to any apparent cause. But he had set in motion a gentle and irreversible sequence. As he succumbed to the substances he had taken, the noose tightened and my son slipped away from the travails of his time on earth.

When Garrett didn't show up for classes Monday, one of his friends wondered why and went by his apartment afterward. He got no response to rapping on the door, but he heard an agitated Oliver whining inside. So he let himself in to see if he could help. Unleashed, the dog dashed from the kitchen to the bedroom and then to the closet to find Garrett. His friend followed and made the discovery that haunts me every day, a discovery that forever fills me with emptiness.

FOURTEEN

Though the rays of morning light streamed into the windows of Garrett's Maryland bedroom, on what would have been his twenty-second birthday, the world never looked darker to me. I wondered if I'd ever know joy again, ever be able to smile at strangers and laugh with friends. Sleepless and sobbing all night long, my grieving had left me disconsolate and despairing. I envied the dead. All I knew was that my beloved and beautiful boy was gone and I couldn't go on. I was a failure at family and nothing else seemed to matter anymore.

Sharon was suffering as well, but she's a stronger person than I am. She had somehow found the emotional strength to greet the day, but I still hadn't. Alarmed by the extent of my collapse, she finally asked our Bethesda bishop, Brad Coltin, to come over to coax me out of Garrett's bed, which they did. Though exhausted, I found energy enough to pack for Pendleton. We had to get Garrett home.

Soon, John Easton, my chief of staff, and Sue Keenom, my assistant, arrived at the house. Sue had made travel arrangements for our return to Oregon and John needed to know how we, as public people, wanted to share the news of our private loss. With no forethought, I grabbed a piece of paper and wrote out: "After years of psychological suffering from deep depression, our son, Garrett Lee Smith, took his life to end his emotional pain." I handed my scribbling to John, saying, "Let's just tell the tragic truth about my boy."

The phone was ringing off the hook now, with family and friends wanting to help, but I couldn't speak to them yet. Then the doorbell rang and standing in the doorway was Oklahoma senator Don Nickles and his wife, Linda. They had been with us at the conference in Ireland and England and had gotten to know Garrett in London. What I did not know until that moment was how well Don knew what I was suffering—his father, he told me, had also committed suicide. He knew the hurt and, as soon as he had heard the news about Garrett, had hurried to our home. As a friend and colleague, Don encouraged me to hold on and told me that, while the pain would never completely go away, fond memories of Garrett would in time make it manageable. I will never forget the extra-mile thoughtfulness of Don and Linda.

When they left, a phone call came that I had to compose myself to take, and Sharon joined me on the line. It was from Gordon B. Hinckley, President of the Church of Jesus Christ of Latter-Day Saints, the earthly leader of our religious faith. He told us that, while he did not know Garrett, our Father in heaven did; that God understood Garrett's capacities and limitations, his afflictions and infirmities, his heart and mind. He assured us that Garrett was in the arms of his Heavenly Father, and that his mind was now calm and clear. He reminded us that the Lord himself had suffered all things in the flesh, even our pains and sicknesses, so that he could care for us all, even Garrett, in the courts of mercy and justice.

Sharon was profoundly comforted by President Hinckley's call, as was I, and we will always treasure his thoughtfulness and timely counsel. It even fortified me for a time, until the flight home. When airborne for Oregon, the flight attendant told me there was an emergency call for me and that I could take it on the pilot's phone. The call was from my brother, Milan, in Los Angeles. He had been working with the authorities in Utah and making arrangements to bring Garrett to Oregon. He had questions I needed to answer and afterward told me that the investigating officer had faxed to him Garrett's suicide note, remarking that in his opinion it revealed "a young man who suffered from a classic case of bipolar disorder." I asked Milan to read me Garrett's last words, and they were consistent with what I had seen in Garrett and heard from him before, revealing the roller coaster of his mind and emotions—great heights, steep descents, and dark tunnels.

My heart broke all over again, even though his words to Sharon and me were filled with kindness: "If it is any consolation, your love is the only thing in my life I know will never change. I'd simply like to feel the same about myself. I love you so much. And just think: your son won't feel that everyday pain anymore. I just wish I could love myself as you love me."

Again I began blaming myself. Why hadn't I been there more for him? Why had I been away from home so much? Why hadn't family life in my home conferred upon him mental health and self-esteem? How was it that my words of encouragement, my prayers earnestly expressed, and the latest in medical prescriptions and counseling had failed to help my son? I struggled with those questions as we flew west. The answers did not come. All I knew was that my son was dead, and I was dying inside.

When we arrived at our Pendleton home, we were touched and amazed to find twenty or so of our friends and neighbors waiting for us in the driveway. From that moment through Garrett's funeral and beyond, the good people of Pendleton have provided a shoulder for Sharon and me to lean on. Soon after we went inside the house, we were told that President George W. Bush was on the phone, and in his wonderful way, as my friend, he did his best to comfort me, encouraging me to come back to Washington when I felt I was able. Sometime later, when President Clinton learned about Garrett, he also called to express sympathy and to share his experiences in sorrow over the loss of loved ones to suicide.

In retrospect, I marvel at the extraordinary ability of these two presidents to sympathize and empathize with those who mourn a lost loved one. Both did so differently, but effectively. Their high office requires them too frequently to be not only commander in chief but mourner in chief. I also learned in my travail that human suffering and family tragedy causes pettiness and partisanship to evaporate like frost in morning light. Pain and loss do not register as Republican or Democrat. They come to all. They are part of our human condition, the suffering and the comforting.

While I had often been called upon to comfort others, I was emotionally unprepared to receive the well-wishers reaching out to me, and in the week between Garrett's death and burial, I unwisely sought out too much isolation. I wandered aimlessly about Pendleton, took long drives in the country, and barricaded myself in my cabin in the aptly named Blue Mountains. My tears and self-torture seemed inexhaustible, and my thinking became twisted and counterproductive. The church leader of my youth, David O. McKay, had once warned, "No other worldly success can compensate for failure in the home." Even this piece of wisdom I turned on myself as a dagger, as yet unable to see that Garrett had become mentally ill, that his manic depression was as lethal to him as any fatal disease.

I began to feel that I should resign from the Senate, return to Oregon, and focus all my time and attention on Brittany and Morgan. After all, I still had two more chances to get it right. I went so far as to e-mail this intention to my chief of staff, John Easton, who was still in Washington holding my Senate staff together. But even as I did this, I knew deep down—something that Sharon kept reminding me—that to resign my seat was the last thing that Garrett, or Brittany and Morgan, would want. But I was bereft, bleeding emotionally, and not thinking rationally.

Many tried to talk sense into me, and one finally did. James E. Faust, Second Counselor to Gordon B. Hinckley, is a most esteemed leader in our church. He is a man of much learning and deep wisdom, long in experience in service to others. Before his years in high church office, he had a distinguished legal career, serving as president of the Utah Bar Association and as state representative in the Utah Legislature. He was also a Democrat. Why I, an Oregon Republican, was so much on his mind, I will never know. But on three occasions during this terrible week he called—first to console, then to counsel, and finally to correct.

On the third call he told me he felt moved to inquire about my feelings and intentions. Honored, yet embarrassed, that this great man would be so concerned about me, I felt he deserved an honest response. I shared with him my thoughts about resignation, at which point he did what I truly needed. He verbally grabbed me by the lapels and gave me a good shaking.

"That's what I thought you'd say," he responded. "Now I want you to listen to me, Senator, and you listen to me good! The devil knows you're down and you've just given me his line. You need to fully grieve for Garrett and get back to work! You are needed, and your children need more than your time, they need most to see your good example, especially now!"

It was straight talk and hard medicine, but from that moment on, I banished any thought of resignation and began to regain my emotional stability. Though tears continued to flow, I could see more clearly my responsibilities, as a parent and to the public.

In preparation for Garrett's burial, Kelly Brown, David Stoddard, and Kent Perkes agreed to dress my boy's body in clothing appropriate for his funeral. Each of them serve in positions of responsibility in my company as well as in ecclesiastical positions in our church. They left the last few buttons and bows for me to do and asked if I was up to the task. I told them I thought I was and met them at the funeral home.

But, when I saw Garrett's lifeless body for the first time, a torrent of memory crashed into my mind: the baby I had cradled, the boy I had bounced on my knee, the bike I had taught him to ride, the books we'd read together, his playing the role of Pecos Bill in a school drama, his bruises after football practice, the times of tears and cheers, Halloweens and Christmas mornings, his Eagle Scout Court of Honor, his high school diploma, and the triumphant return from England—all ashes now in my memory.

I flooded his clothing with bittersweet tears and held him tight for a time, unable to fasten a button or tie a bow. Kelly, the father of Garrett's friend, Ethan, held me up and hauled me out as I collapsed again in grief. But, having done this, and having seen with my own eyes that Garrett was gone, strangely strengthened me for the funeral.

Seven days had passed and the day of Garrett's memorial service arrived, a Monday. We had decided to hold a private service in the chapel where I had once presided as bishop, and where Garrett had been baptized and learned the Gospel basics. We made no public announcement of the services, but the public came anyway, and they were most welcome.

They filled up the chapel, the annex hall, and the crowd finally overflowed into the hallways and the sidewalks outside. The whole community was in pain and wanted to be present. Garrett's friends, coaches, teachers, customers from the gasoline station, scoutmasters, and mission companions came from as far away as Russia and Bulgaria. How I wish Garrett could have seen the difference he had made in so many lives.

Affection for Sharon and me also came, from every time and clime of our lives, from every corner of Oregon and the country, even from around the world. Boyhood friends, college roommates, New Zealand missionaries, law and business associates, labor and management, lawmakers, political advisors, farmers and ranchers, Christians and Jews, the churched and the unchurched all gathered in that little Mormon chapel on Pendleton's north hill to pay respect to Garrett and to help us heal. I shall never forget them, their thoughtfulness, every one.

Dr. Bill Frist, the Senate majority leader, had the flags lowered over the Capitol and closed down Senate business, so that my colleagues and their spouses could attend the funeral. Alaska senator Ted Stevens led the delegation, which was remarkable in itself, because just a short time earlier I had resisted his pleas to vote in favor of allowing oil drilling in Alaska's Arctic National Wildlife Reserve. But, as Ted reminded me, when he had lost his wife in a plane crash early in his Senate career, the comfort of his colleagues was crucial in his own recovery. Also present were Ohio senator Mike DeWine and his wife, Fran, themselves experienced in grief after losing a daughter in an automobile accident. Senator Bob and Joyce Bennett of Utah, and Senator Saxby Chambliss of Georgia also gathered around us to offer support. Nevada senator Harry Reid and his wife, Landra, led the Democrats. Senator Reid was another colleague who understood what we were suffering: his father had committed suicide as a consequence of depression. My Oregon colleague, Ron Wyden, was there, no doubt remembering the recent death of his brother, who had suffered from schizophrenia. Sitting near him was my Oregon congressman, Greg Walden, and his wife, Mylene, who had lost a son in infancy.

It is unlikely that little Pendleton, Oregon, had ever seen in a single day so large a concentration of congressional power. But those gathered in that chapel came not to exercise power. Rather, they came to show compassion and to share in our suffering. The good they gave us also taught me that the expression of care and kindness costs us little more than our time, and its effects last forever.

The music and the remarks made during the service were heartbreaking and beautiful. Garrett's mission president, Philip Wightman, and Ralph W. Hardy Jr., a lifelong family friend and a respected leader in the church, gave stirring and strengthening remarks; sufficient, so that at the service's conclusion, I found it possible to speak and express gratitude to Sharon—Garrett's "angel mother"—and for everything each person in that overflow assembly had done for Garrett during his short life, and for us in our grief. I also promised that I would soon go back to work and would yet identify some good out of Garrett's tragedy. When I promised this, I scarcely imagined how obsessed I would become in finding that "good" over the coming year.

We buried Garrett on a green hill at the base of the Blue Mountains, overlooking the pioneer town of Weston, Oregon, and the Walla Walla valley, close to the location of Smith Frozen Foods. I had admired the beauty and serenity of this place for years, as it was. Its graves date back to the 1860s. Ironically, I had pointed out this place to Garrett one weekend when he had come home to get his car and had made him promise that he'd put me there when I passed away. He promised he would and seemed pleased by the site. I never imagined I'd take him there first. But now, whenever I go home to Pendleton, I go there as well, to find peace and to ponder eternal things. I usually also leave a long-stem English red rose in remembrance of my son and place it in front of the rough-hewn granite headstone I had fashioned for him, emblematic of his unfinished life.

I tell all of this because there is no owner's manual for burying one's child. Each must do it in a way that helps them cope. This is how I cope. No matter the cause of a child's death, it is, I believe, life's greatest and most painful test, perhaps because it is so unnatural, so out of season. Something primal within us teaches that we are not supposed to outlive our children, that we are to shepherd them all of our days. But, when the wolf arrives, sometimes we cannot save them and the pain is sharp and piercing.

Forgive me for imagining also that when the cause of a child's death is suicide, a parent's remorse is extra cruel. In the months following Garrett's interment, the word *why* captured my every waking thought. The extreme devastation and intense grief of the week between his death and burial were now replaced by overwhelming bewilderment and shame and sadness.

These feelings were reaffirmed when I happened to glance at a pamphlet to parents that listed warning signs that may precede a child's suicide. Those signs included trouble sleeping, drastic changes in behavior, giving away prized possessions, taking unnecessary risks, losing interest in personal appearance, alcohol abuse, feelings of worthlessness and hopelessness, and excessive anxiety and impulsivity. To my dismay and self-disgust, Garrett had, at one time or another, manifested all of these signs, but until that night in Scotland, I had not known of their ominous portent.

As Sharon and I set about to settle Garrett's affairs and to get Brittany and Morgan on with life and back to school, I was physically enervated and emotionally exhausted. Thankfully,

Kelly and Ethan Brown, along with David Stoddard, offered to pack up and move out Garrett's belongings from his college apartment. Neither Sharon nor I felt we could go back to that place, but we did travel to Provo, to reconstruct as best we could what had happened and "why."

Debriefing with Garrett's psychiatrist was especially helpful and enlightening. When the doctor asked me if I had any questions for him, I asked, "Was I complicit in killing my son?" Had I, through traveling, striving, and achieving throughout Garrett's life, created too much turmoil in his mind and in his life, set standards too high for him to reach, and crippled him emotionally with my expectations?

"Absolutely not!" he responded emphatically. "If your work had you home every night and made you a couch potato on the weekends, he would still be dead."

He begged me to believe that Garrett had not killed himself to hurt me or because of me, but because he was gravely ill, most likely manic-depressive. Sufferers of this debilitating malady often have a chemical imbalance of the brain because of insufficient serotonin, a neurotransmitter that helps control mood and the mind. Such conditions are often lethal because they create in the sufferer mental anguish that can no longer be endured, a despair that goes beyond despair, unimaginable to those who have never experienced it. I wanted to believe him, but still I wondered.

Greater insight into Garrett's state of mind in his final days would come months later when we received a letter from Loreena McGibbon, a lovely young British woman who had become engaged to one of Garrett's British mission companions. During that final trip to England with Garrett, he had confided to her some of his deepest feelings and dangerous fears, his sense of hopelessness and his struggle to get beyond the darkness that terrorized him. Loreena wrote, "From what I can gather, Garrett had reached a stage in his life where he knew the illness would come to play a part in other people's futures—the person he would marry and his children. I know he couldn't stand the thought that an action he took at some future point would possibly leave them missing a husband and father." Loreena's letter rang true to Sharon and me because it captured the true essence of our son—the Garrett who was always thinking of others.

When we returned to Washington, I had been away for

nearly three weeks and had missed many Senate votes. I hoped my constituents in Oregon would understand and that they would soon see that I had kept my promise to go back to work. However, for several months more, I was emotionally fragile, mentally unmotivated, and physically lethargic. Facing friends and colleagues was psychologically strenuous. Each day it felt like an anvil was on my heart and, at unexpected and embarrassing times, the blacksmith would begin banging away. On these occasions, I'd have to walk out of a Senate hearing, excuse myself from a meal, or end a speech early to find a private place to let, once again, grief wash over me like a wave.

I buried many personal ambitions along with Garrett. I abandoned plans to run for a Senate Republican Conference leadership position and concluded that my best option was to plod along and try to recapture my old passion for the political contest. To do otherwise, I realized, was unfair to Oregon, because in the aggressive environs of the United States Senate, a senator and his state can get run over if he is not fully engaged.

In reality, my colleagues were wonderful and helpful. Each found a way to put an emotional arm around me. Senator Frist would talk me through the medical realities of our experience.

Senator Tom Daschle, the Democrat leader, also showed genuine concern and desired to help. Orrin Hatch sent a long and heartfelt handwritten letter to express his feelings for Sharon and me and about Garrett. Hillary Clinton took me for a long walk to talk things over. Ted Kennedy approached me repeatedly, eyes brimming with tears, unable to speak. Few families have suffered more tragedy than the Kennedys, and his tears said all that needed to be said. Joe Biden also proved a real brother. On three occasions he pulled me down into a Senate chair next to him to counsel me about grief. He knew the subject intimately, as his wife and his daughter had been taken from him in a traffic accident just weeks after his first election to the Senate in 1972. Pat Leahy and Rick Santorum had candles lit for us in Catholic parishes. Dianne Feinstein and Elizabeth Dole were among those donating generously to Garrett's memorial fund, Joe Lieberman remembered us in his synagogue, and many Protestant colleagues included us in their prayer circles. I was reminded over and over again that human heartache has no political or religious affiliation.

Perhaps the most practical piece of advice I received for dealing with day-to-day doses of guilt and grief came from the retired chaplain of the United States Senate, Dr. Lloyd John Ogilvie. Reverend Ogilvie had long pastored the historic First Presbyterian Church of Hollywood, California, and when he spoke, his melodious and penetrating voice made you imagine that you were hearing the voice of God Himself. Lloyd had recently lost his lovely wife, Mary Jane, to an illness and he called me from Los Angeles to commiserate. His message to me was that "gratitude" is a miraculous antidote for grief, and that, whenever I was feeling overwhelmed by bewilderment and remorse, I should remember to be grateful that the Lord gave us Garrett for twenty-two years less a day. Through this recollection, the clouds of melancholy would soon pass and be replaced by smiles and fond memories of my son. It sounded simple enough—gratitude as an antidote for grief—so I tried it. And I've tried it many times since, because it works! I have found that gratitude can banish grief and make confusing emotions manageable.

FIFTEEN

In addition to faith and the fellowship of friends, learning about mental illness also helped to ease the pain of losing Garrett. As is now apparent, I knew little about psychology from my schooling. But now I needed to learn emotionally; I wanted to be certain that what Garrett's doctor had told me was true—that there was nothing Sharon and I could have said or done to help our son to love and value himself and to find happiness in his search, instead of death.

By chance, former Oregon senator Bob Packwood stopped me one day in the Capitol and told me he had a friend he wanted me to meet. I appreciated his thoughtfulness and agreed to a meeting. At the appointed time he came to my office and introduced Sharon and me to Kay Redfield Jamison, a professor of psychiatry at Baltimore's Johns Hopkins University, herself bipolar and a survivor of an attempted suicide. I didn't know then that she is one of the world's foremost authorities on the psychology of suicide. And I didn't recognize until later what a revelation her remarkable writings on the subject would become for me.

Sharon gave Garrett's suicide note to Kay and, as she read it, I sat before her as an empty vessel, not knowing what to say or what to ask. Over the next hour, she filled me with knowledge and understanding and, best of all, began unpacking my baggage of guilt.

With her help, I started to build an intellectual foundation for understanding what she termed "suicide's ability to undermine, overwhelm, outwit, devastate, and destroy" my son. She taught us that the unimaginable mental pain from illnesses like Garrett's makes self-destruction seem the only escape, that "suicide is not beholden to an evening's promise, nor does it always harken to plans drawn up in lucid moments and banked in good intentions." For anyone, and particularly any parent, dealing with a circumstance of mental illness, Jamison's books, *Night Falls Fast* and *An Unquiet Mind,* should be required reading.

Beyond the confines of Capitol Hill and the good people of Pendleton, thousands wrote to express sympathy and to share their stories of mental illness or a family member's suicide. As a result of the publicity surrounding Garrett's death, we had become the focus of an immense fraternity of sorrow. I had never been aware of or imagined the size of this silent and shapeless society, but the avalanche of letters confirmed what my studies later taught me: There are 30,000 suicides and as many as 600,000 attempts of suicide in America every year. Suicide is the third leading cause of death in the United States for those ages fifteen to twenty-four. It is the second leading cause of death among college students, with more than a thousand taking their own lives each year. Many estimate that the number of suicides and attempted suicides for young people is actually two to five times higher because so many go unreported or are covered up because of the stigma associated with suicide. I began to realize that I was sitting on top of a mountain of remorse and wondered what I, as a United States Senator, could do about it. After all, wasn't that why I'd wanted to become a senator in the first place—to do good?

The first official public events in Oregon in which I took part following Garrett's death strengthened my growing resolve to find a difference I could make. Early in my first term, I had intervened with the federal bureaucracy to make possible the construction and operation of a new hospital in the rural community of Cottage Grove. City leaders had planned the dedication ceremonies of the hospital around my schedule in order for me to attend, but in light of Garrett's death, they assured my office that they would completely understand if I was unable to honor the commitment. To the contrary, however, I felt it necessary to determine whether I had the emotional stamina to face Oregonians again, just as I had my colleagues on Capitol Hill.

It didn't take long for me to realize that the people of Oregon were incredibly supportive and remarkably understanding. Regardless of their political party or philosophy, it seemed that everyone wanted to whisper a kind word in my ear, to put an arm around my shoulder, and to tell me—many with tears in their eyes—that they were thinking of and praying for Sharon and me. While I was touring the hospital, a number of nurses and doctors also made a point of pointing out that mental-health issues had been ignored in America for too long.

Later that same day, I attended a gathering at the Eugene, Oregon, home of Dave Frohnmayer, the president of the University of Oregon. Before other university officials arrived, Dave took me into his study for a private conversation. I knew that Dave and his wife, Lynn, had lost two of their daughters to Fanconi's anemia, a congenital disease. They had become courageous national and international leaders in the effort to find a cure for the disease, and Dave told me how channeling their grief into this mission had helped them to persevere. After Dave and I joined the other guests, the university's dean of students shook my hand and thanked me for publicly discussing Garrett's suicide. She told me that calls to the student health services center on campus had dramatically increased in the days following Garrett's death. She believed that our forthright decision to publicly state that Garrett had taken his own life had led other college students to seek help, fearing they were suffering

"Garrett Smith's problem." I left Eugene determined to find meaning in Garrett's life by doing everything in my power to help others who were afflicted as he was.

The generosity of friends and strangers in Oregon and across the country allowed Sharon and me an opportunity to do just that. Monetary contributions poured in to the Garrett Lee Smith Memorial Fund we had established at St. Anthony's Hospital in Pendleton. This facility of Catholic healing and charity is where my mother gave birth to me and six of my nine siblings, and the place to which we rushed Garrett for his share of emergencies and boyhood stitches. More than $100,000 was contributed to the memorial fund and the funds have been used to endow a mental-health center at St. Anthony's. A library resource and reading room has been created, computers and software purchased, a web page placed on line, and diagnostic tools using Columbia University's innovative TeenScreen program made available to Pendleton's public schools. Rebecca Thomas of my Oregon staff also worked with the hospital to create a beautiful collage of Garrett's life. We have dedicated this center to hope, help, and healing and named it in Garrett's honor. The dedication was a heartwarming community celebration and I feel certain that, over time, this facility will help identify danger signals, intervene, and save the lives of hundreds of struggling souls.

But as the cascade of correspondence proved, the problem extended far beyond Pendleton and Oregon. Depression-induced suicide was a crisis, an epidemic, across America, especially on college campuses, and I needed to do something more. But what?

Six months after Garrett's death, Ohio Senator Mike DeWine provided me with a legislative answer. He told me that the epidemic of youth suicides had been weighing on his mind, as well, and that he had coauthored two pieces of legislation that he hoped might make a positive difference. The first bill, which he'd authored with Senator Chris Dodd of Connecticut, would increase screening for children to detect those predisposed to depression and suicide. Studies have shown that the earlier such a predisposition is diagnosed, the better the chance of treating it successfully, and saving a life.

The second bill, written with Senator Jack Reed of Rhode Island, would provide funding necessary to improve suicide-prevention programs on college campuses. I reviewed the two bills, feeling more and more that not only had I found my cause, but I'd discovered a new passion and reason for continuing my service in the Senate. I may not have known much about psychology, but I knew the law and how to make it.

Senator DeWine told me that he would soon be chairing a hearing on the two bills in the Senate Health, Education, Labor, and Pensions Committee and asked whether I was emotionally able to come before the committee and tell Garrett's story. I told him that I'd try and I'd do all I could to support his bills. But he offered me something more. He said he'd take a backseat, and let me be the driving force behind moving the bills through Congress. Senators Dodd and Reed agreed and promised that they would be there to help whenever it was needed. They were wonderful throughout the journey.

The night before the hearing, I stayed late at my Senate office and handwrote on a legal pad an abbreviated version of Garrett's story. The next morning, Sharon and I shuffled into the solemn, wood-paneled hearing room, filled to overflowing and banked with television and print reporters. Senator Wyden and several of my staff members sat directly behind us to offer moral support. When Senator DeWine gaveled the hearing to order, he was joined on the committee dais by Senators Dodd, Kennedy, Clinton, and Tom Harkin. After their opening statements, I was invited to testify. The subject and the setting led me to simply read what I'd written and hold on, as best I could, to my raw emotional wounds. I did it poorly and twice had to stop for extended periods to compose myself. But I got through it and concluded with a line from Norman Maclean's poignant family story, *A River Runs Through It:* "It is those we live with and love, and should know, who elude us." But I got through it and continued, "That Garrett eluded me haunts me every day, and no doubt will for the rest of my days. But this much I know—that he was a beautiful boy and that I loved him completely without completely understanding him."

As my words trailed off, the stunned silence that filled the large room was interrupted only by the sounds of sniffling and sobs. Senator Kennedy said tearfully, "Mr. Chairman, I think we're all just overwhelmed." Senator Dodd added, "If the 108th Congress accomplishes nothing else, we ought to at least pass this legislation into law."

SIXTEEN

M y next six months in the Senate were like a seminar in "Civics 101": the separation of powers between the White House and Capitol Hill, the checks and balances between the House of Representatives and the Senate, the power of committee chairmen, the maneuvering of staffers, competition for time on the legislative calendar, the unending conflict between Republicans and Democrats, and the clash between conservatism and liberalism—all these elements crashed together during my efforts to pass the legislation my colleagues had placed in my care.

I had authored many bills and amendments and won hundreds of appropriations before, but usually I included them on session-ending omnibus bills or attached them to other must-pass legislative vehicles. Passing a stand-alone law is arduous in the American federal system, and doing so, while keeping Oregon's other concerns moving as well, occupied all my concentration.

Fortunately I was aided by a remarkable individual, Catherine Finley, whom I had recently hired to help me with Finance Committee matters. Her talent, tenacity, and temperament were just what I needed for completing a tall order in a short time. My personal timetable for this task was to have it completed by what would have been Garrett's twenty-third birthday, September 9, 2004. But when President Bush learned of my efforts to pass legislation targeting youth suicide, he expressed his support and asked that I get the bill to him by the August recess, so he could honor Garrett and us by traveling to Oregon—perhaps even Pendleton—to sign it.

With the President's support, the White House Council on Mental Health weighed in with a number of improvements to the legislation, as did experts from the Substance Abuse and Mental Health Administration. Mental-health advocacy organizations also made suggestions and offered their full support, mobilizing their members behind the cause. Senator Judd Gregg of New Hampshire, the chairman of the Senate Health, Education, Labor, and Pensions Committee, added some constructive changes, combined the two bills into one piece of legislation, and promised to move it to the Senate floor. Without my knowing, Senator DeWine moved that the combined bill be named the "Garrett Lee Smith Memorial Act." When I learned of this, I teared up again. I also felt that if goodness were ever packaged in human form, it would look like Mike DeWine.

Leaders Frist and Daschle had been so supportive of my efforts from the beginning and, perhaps seeing the bill as a bipartisan chance to lower the political temperature for a moment, they quickly scheduled it for debate and a vote on the floor of the Senate. Sympathy and encouragement from colleagues on both sides of the aisle, along with the mobilization of mental-health professionals and advocacy groups, made passage a certainty.

The media also helped to raise awareness of the issue. My testimony before the HELP Committee had caught the attention of ABC's Ted Koppel, who featured it on an episode of *Nightline* that focused on depression and suicide. Kay Redfield Jamison and CBS newsman Mike Wallace, who had movingly written about his own battle with depression, appeared with me on the program.

When the bill reached the Senate floor, I prayed that I'd be in better control of my emotions. But I was not. It still hurt too much and I was too caught up in the emotion of this cause. I'm grateful that the C-Span camera respectfully panned away from me while I struggled to regain my composure. Some of my colleagues also wrestled with their emotions. Harry Reid and Don Nickles delivered eloquent remarks, and both shared the fact that they had lost their fathers to suicide. The vote to pass Garrett's bill was unanimous, and the raw reality of the evening caught the attention of the media. The following morning, I was invited to appear on NBC's *Today Show* to explain what Garrett's bill would accomplish should it become law. When Katie Couric asked me to predict what would happen next, I said that I was confident that House members would also see the positive results that would come from this legislation, and that passage there would prove that preventing youth suicide was a bicameral as well as a bipartisan cause. In the end, it was, but getting to the end was more tortured and twisted than I had ever imagined.

My first call in the House was to Congressman Tom Osborne of Nebraska, who had previously agreed to be the lead sponsor in his chamber. Congressman Osborne had gained fame as the longtime football coach at the University of Nebraska and had seen a number of suicides on the Cornhusker campus. Tom was ready to move full speed ahead, and he'd enlisted the support of Congressman Bart Gordon, a Democrat from Tennessee, the ranking member of the House Commerce Committee, where the bill had been assigned for a hearing.

Bart then accompanied me to a meeting with the committee chairman, Congressman Joe Barton of Texas. Chairman Barton was interested and sympathetic from the outset and said that he looked forward to working with me. He also reminded me, however, that the House was a coequal branch with the Senate, and that I would have to be amenable to making changes in the legislation should his colleagues demand them. I assured him that I knew the Senate was not the font of all wisdom, and I welcomed improvements to the legislation.

Tom Osborne then arranged a meeting with Speaker of the House Dennis Hastert. Speaker Hastert was a former high school teacher and wrestling coach. Like Tom, his years of working with kids led him to immediately grasp the value of the bill. But he also bluntly told me that if I wanted the bill to pass, I'd have to satisfy the demands of Chairman Barton.

My next visit was to House Majority Leader Tom DeLay of Texas. He was sympathetic but seemed unconvinced of the need for or the merits of the legislation. Nevertheless, his counsel was essentially the same as the Speaker's—satisfy Joe Barton and he wouldn't obstruct a House vote. My marching orders in hand, I went to work and spent the better part of two months on the House side of Capitol Hill. This involved negotiating differences, reconciling revisions, pleading with and cajoling representatives, and at times even groveling.

I soon learned that a group of congressmen called the Republican Study Group had a virtual stranglehold on legislation that was to come to the floor for a vote by the full House of Representatives. Members of this group were often referred to as "CATS," an acronym derived from the group's former name—Conservative Action Team. The CATS showed their claws early, hitting Chairman Barton with one demand after another for changes to Garrett's bill, many of which seemed to be born of ignorance or ideological hard-heartedness.

I began approaching the objecting congressmen individually in the hope of addressing their concerns and was appalled by some of their responses. "Your bill has Democrat sponsors," said one. "We don't pass bills over here that Democrats want!" Another member told me that stopping kids from preventing suicide was the business of parents and not the federal government. "But what if the parents don't know any better?" I asked. "Can't the government help?" I pointed out that the government rightfully spends hundreds of millions of dollars in an effort to find cures for diseases and improve physical health. Why couldn't it also play a role in issues involving mental health? I could tell by the uncomprehending look on one congressman's face that he didn't understand the point I was trying to make, a point I knew only too painfully and too late.

In successive conversations with two other members, I heard one complain that the $83 million the bill authorized to fund suicide-prevention programs was too much money, and the other tell me that it was not enough money to make a difference. I conceded to the one that more money would save more kids but insisted that it was a good beginning upon which we could build. Another congressman chimed in, "We're at war, Senator. You need to stay focused on providing for the common defense!" I asked him, "So we should just forget about domestic tranquility and promoting the general welfare?" I tried reasoning with him, explaining that the responsibilities of the federal government were not mutually exclusive and that we were perfectly capable of meeting foreign threats and domestic obligations at the same time.

The last straw came when, as the annual August recess neared, I approached several CATS whom I had helped or worked with during my years in the Senate, and who I regarded as friends. Under the rules of the House, the only way to get the bill passed in the days before the recess was through a procedure called the Executive Calendar, which expedited consideration of noncontroversial legislation. I shared with them the President's desire to sign the bill in Oregon during the August recess and asked whether they would agree to the expedited process. They declined to help, promising to object to any attempt by their leaders to "fast-track" the bill, thereby ensuring that a final vote on the bill could not take place until Congress returned to session in September. One tried to soften his refusal, saying, "Don't take this personally. This is just politics."

"It's hard not to take it personally," I replied, "when the bill is named after your dead son!"

I stormed back to the Senate, grieving again, deeply disappointed, and even incensed, but I refused to give up. I asked Senator Rick Santorum of Pennsylvania, a former House member held in high regard by many members of the CATS, to do what he could to convince them to bring the bill up for a vote before the recess. They ignored his request. Faced with the opposition of the CATS, Chairman Barton called me to apologize that he couldn't move the bill in time to meet the President's timetable. He promised to bring Garrett's bill up as the first order of business when Congress returned. I was grateful for Joe's promise, but I worried that the CATS would spend August plotting new ways to make mischief.

When I went home that night, I was angry and embarrassed that members of my own party could be so callous and counterproductive. Sharon tried to console me and said, "You can only do what you can do. Garrett knows you tried." I hoped that Garrett also knew that Sharon was doing all she could, too. She had become an advocate for the TeenScreen program, and she had accepted a gracious offer from Ted Kulongoski, the governor of Oregon, to serve on his Mental Health Task Force.

The President still came to Oregon that August, but no bill was signed. I thanked him for being a compassionate conservative and for all the help I had received from the White House legislative staff. They had been wonderful, I told him, and in my corner the whole time. He responded philosophically, saying, "Senator, your bill is a good bill and it will make good law, and it will be my privilege to sign it soon." I was comforted by his confidence and am always inspired by his persistence and determination to do what is right, as he sees the right, no matter the storms ahead. He is my friend and I am his.

When the Congress reconvened after Labor Day 2004, my worries were confirmed. Intending to scuttle the bill, the CATS had a final demand of Chairman Barton, which was a potential poison pill. The concept of parental notification in federal education programs gives parents the right to opt a child out of a program. For mental-health screenings, however, the CATS wanted it reversed—requiring parents to affirmatively opt a child into the program. While I also supported parental rights, I knew this would likely reduce the numbers of children tested. This change greatly alarmed House Democrats who feared this precedent would bleed into other education programs, and some began to waver in their support of the bill. I suspected this was precisely what the CATS had intended. Since they knew their opposition wasn't enough to defeat the bill, they were hoping to find a way to make it as unappealing as they could to other members. If the Democrats turned against the bill, then, coupled with CATS' opposition, they could defeat the bill and pin the blame on the Democrats. Thankfully, Chairman Barton added language making it clear that the "opt in" provision only applied to Garrett's bill, and not to other education programs.

I called Congressman Pat Kennedy, Ted's son, who, like his dad, is a champion of mental-health legislation, and explained what was happening, why he needn't worry, and why I needed him to hold on to the Democrats. He understood completely and promised to do his best to keep his colleagues on board. I also called two members of the Oregon House delegation, Democrat Earl Blumenauer and Republican Greg Walden, and explained the same to them. Both of these colleagues are real workhorses and proved themselves to be champions of the bill from beginning to end.

The final House vote on the Garrett Lee Smith Act took place on September 9, 2004—what would have been Garrett's twenty-third birthday. Chairman Barton spoke for the bill accurately and persuasively, as did my Oregon friends, Congressmen Blumenauer and Walden, and my House sponsors, Bart Gordon and Tom Osborne. When the vote was called, Garrett won in a landslide, along with untold thousands who suffer as he did. House Republicans and Democrats joined together in an overwhelming victory. When the speaker brought down the gavel, my tears came down as well.

That evening, when the House presented its version of the Garrett Lee Smith Memorial Act to the Senate, Majority Leader Frist moved immediately for its passage. I was given time to speak and, this time, did so without tears. I remembered the advice of Chaplain Ogilvie, and my words were of gratitude, not of grief. The vote was unanimous—one of the few in an acrimonious political season. The hardest legislative battle I ever fought was over—and won.

As colleagues gathered around to clasp my hand and express congratulations, I could not help but wonder what Garrett must be thinking. A year ago he had written, "Put me in the ground and forget about me"—but that night the Republicans and Democrats of the 108th Congress, acting as Americans, had affixed his name to a new statute of the United States. As I walked away from the Senate that evening, I paused for a moment and looked heavenward into the starry night. Everything was in its place, the planets, the constellations, the galaxies, the North Star still pointing true. Perhaps part of Garrett's purpose in life, I wondered, was to help his father to understand and to achieve this for him and for others. I was at peace, and I said simply into the vast blue above, "Happy Birthday, son."

SEVENTEEN

The 2004 campaign for President of the United States was in full fever by September. Every charge and counter-charge burned hot, the stakes were high, and America seemed consumed by the contest. For me, however, the most unforgettable moment of that campaign season was a little-noticed private White House ceremony where partisanship was temporarily set aside, and where a Republican President and some of his most vocal Democrat critics stood side by side in common cause.

The final step in making American law is a simple and solemn act: the President signs his name to the statute. This was done for the Garrett Lee Smith Memorial Act on the morning of October 21, 2004. Misty weather caused us to move from the Rose Garden to the Roosevelt Room, indoors. The White House had invited Sharon, Brittany, Morgan, and me, and asked us to invite a few friends, mental-health advocates, and key congressional supporters of Garrett's bill. Most of my Capitol Hill colleagues could not attend because of campaign commitments, but those who did were in equal numbers Republicans and Democrats.

When I called Ted Kennedy to invite him to attend, I was in Oregon campaigning for President Bush, and he was in California campaigning for John Kerry. "We're campaigning at cross-purposes, Ted," I said, "but I want to invite you to the signing ceremony for Garrett's bill."

"I want to be there," he replied immediately. "I'll see if my schedule can be reworked."

He was able to attend, and the atmosphere in that room contained not a hint of factionalism, despite the fractious atmosphere outside. Warm friendships, sincere satisfaction, and quiet celebration were the attitudes of all. I wished that Americans could have seen it. It was a brief but renewing moment for our Republic.

As we awaited the President's arrival, I did not mourn Garrett, I just missed him. Oh, for one more moment with him, *this* moment, I longed. My work, which had taken so much time from him, had now worked in his name. It comforted me to imagine all the young people like Garrett, whose names I'd never know and whose faces I'd never see, whose sufferings might be relieved and whose lives might be spared through the assistance provided by his law.

Then the door opened and the President walked in, and he welcomed us warmly. Sharon was holding Garrett's picture and she began to sob. This time, I was calm as a summer's morning, feeling a small sense of absolution. The President hugged Sharon, kissed her cheek, and said, "Don't cry, Momma, we're going to do a wonderful thing here this morning." Then the President sat before a small table, and, with his signature, the Garrett Lee Smith Memorial Act was enshrined in American law.

EPILOGUE

When I was a boy I had many big dreams. But when those dreams ran into difficult realities, I'd run to my mother for consolation. Finding comfort on her shoulder, she would often calmly tell me, "Son, if it doesn't kill you, it will make you stronger." The agony of losing Garrett has often caused me to dust off the memory of her words.

Garrett's death didn't kill me, but it did change me. I comb more gray hair now and the furrow in my brow has deepened. The clock seems to mark time differently, less frantically, and the calendar reorders pressing priorities more carefully. I am glad that my broken heart still beats, that the fog of my spirit has lifted, and that the fire that consumed my mind has gone out. The furnace of affliction burns especially hot when our children are the cause of the flames. Some parents, I have observed, are consumed; others are refined. Time helps but never fully heals, so I am still working on refinement.

Garrett is gone, but never forgotten. I sense his spirit still in the wind whispering through ponderosa pines. I see his smile in the rays of sunrise. I hear his booming laughter in the sounds of summer thunder. I receive these remembrances from nature as Heaven's tender mercies.

Still, I have many regrets—things I wish I'd said, circumstances I could have handled better, information I should have known, and, especially, time I cannot reclaim. My many times of absence have left my treasure trove of memories of Garrett less full than I would like. But the memories that I have, some of which I have shared, are my emeralds, rubies, and sapphires. But time has taught me that to look at these gems too often, or for too long, can dim them in self-pity. Besides, generous Garrett would want me to look outward, to others in need like him.

Were my mother still alive, she would remind me that "pain is inevitable, but misery is optional." I am no longer miserable, in part, no doubt, because my mourning over Garrett followed a fairly predictable, restorative path: catastrophe and chaos, grieving and coping, acceptance and advocacy.

In John Irving's novel *The World According to Garp*, a character laments over the death of his son: "Ever since Walt died, my life has felt like an epilogue." Mine does not. And even so, an epilogue needn't be sad. Nowadays, time with Sharon, Brittany, and Morgan, though still often interrupted by senatorial duties, is more precious than ever. Mortal life is fragile, so every family moment is made to count and be savored. Life without my son persuades me all the more that the most important work any of us will ever do is that which we do at home. It means the most, lasts the longest, and makes the greatest difference. The tallest monuments we build in life, the kind that pigeons can't perch upon, are the human ones we build within the walls of our homes.

It is my privilege and pleasure to work right now in a town filled with monuments to the famous and the dead. Many of these monuments memorialize noble words and deeds and, at the same time, they anesthetize us to our own mutability and mortality. I aspire to no such monument, but I take renewed enjoyment in my service as a United States Senator. In that service, since Garrett's death, my focus has changed, my heart has softened, and my backbone has strengthened. It has been satisfying to resist—on one occasion, by threatening to bring down the entire federal budget—unwise programmatic proposals that would have unraveled Medicaid, food stamps, and other safety-net programs that serve the underprivileged, the elderly, and the disabled.

Underlying my motives in these fights and filibusters is my concern, even alarm, over the issues of mental health. Unlike my family, the poor cannot afford and access many mental-health programs, and such services are often the first to suffer budget cuts. This crucial area of medicine always seems to take a backseat to physical health. But, as Garrett taught me, mental illnesses can be just as dangerous and lethal to health as physical illnesses. My cause is to bring suicide's brutal toll and mental health's subordinate status out of the shadows. The shame and stigma our society feels about mental health must stop, and our national conversation needs to begin. If government policy and insurance priorities do not change, then more lives will be tragically lost, more families will be shattered, more of our citizens will wander our streets and needlessly fill our jails, and higher costs will be borne by taxpayers or be shifted to overburdened private policy holders. In short, our society will be diminished and too many of our fellow citizens will continue to suffer needlessly. That is my cause.

Thus ends Garrett's—and my—story. Yet life goes on, the sun comes up and it goes down. Each day's newspapers scream headlines of catastrophe, collapse, rises and falls, wins and losses, wars and rumors of war. Children go to school and the mailman delivers. The ordinary and the extraordinary bombard us 24/7 in the form of everything from blogs to cable news. Through it all, though damaged by Garrett's death, I was not shattered by it. Perhaps I was even strengthened by this struggle. After surviving the loss of my son, any future sadness or setbacks that await me in my epilogue years seem now easy to endure.

Lastly, there is one more thing that, if I could, I would give to all. It has sustained me throughout my wanderings in mortality's mists. It is the glue that held me together in grieving for Garrett. It does the same for others. That one thing is, simply, faith. Death will come to us all, but faith does not. A faith that life has eternal purpose, that we are not on earth by accident or chance. A faith that can bridge the fearful chasm between mortality and eternity. In the Book of Job, this much-afflicted, long-suffering man poses a timeless, haunting question: "If a man die, shall he live again?" Like Job, and because of faith, I can answer with a resounding shout: Yes!

But still, while in this world, in remembering Garrett, I miss him so. . . .

Gordon H. Smith
March 2006

A MOTHER'S MEMORIES

BY SHARON LANKFORD SMITH

Unlike Gordon, when I look back on my time with Garrett, my treasure trove of memories is overflowing. Garrett was a big part of my life and he always will be. I often feel he is with me and I know that although no love or relationship is perfect, ours was very special.

Ever since I was a little girl my biggest dream was to be a wife and mother. Perhaps I was just a product of the 1950s, but I don't think so. Everyone finds personal contentment and satisfaction in different ways, some in the workplace, others in the community. My greatest joy and fulfillment has always come from my family. Old-fashioned? Maybe, but, honestly, that is who I am.

I am a true believer that you love what you serve. After so many years of hope and anticipation, I felt like I hit the jackpot when I finally became a mother. Motherhood is more than a full-time job, and there is no more demanding service one can give. From early morning to late at night, I was able to be there for Garrett, and I consider this a very special privilege—one I realize not everyone has the chance to experience.

Gordon and I were, and are, a good team. His successes in business and politics allowed me to stay at home and be there for Garrett. Although Gordon was often away, I always felt his love and support for how I handled things at home. I was fortunate not to be overburdened with excessive outside responsibilities, chores, yard work, or trying to make ends meet. After living modestly as a child, life with my husband and children has exceeded my dreams.

There was no way I could have ever known what sheer joy and fulfillment this special son would bring me and all those around him. From the start, Garrett was a child who came so gentle and good-natured that he was so very easy to love and serve. There was always his big smile, laughter, and a twinkle in his eye that was more rewarding than any paycheck could ever be.

I believe our special relationship was able to develop because of some unique circumstances that bonded us. Children have different personalities, and Garrett came to this earth especially loving and easy. He was a kind child, and I could always count on him to be obedient. His thoughtfulness and generosity quickly stood out. Knowing that all children aren't naturally this way, I knew I was a lucky mother. Although there were times when I grew tired, it was easy to do a little more with this appreciative and loving son.

When his learning disability became apparent, I was never overwhelmed, because I knew we could get through it. By this point, it was clear that Garrett was hardworking and never took for granted the help offered him. He would always do his part and was comfortable asking for more when he needed it. Best of all was the appreciation he would express and the great pride he felt when a task was completed.

Garrett loved to talk with anyone who would listen. Some of my favorite memories are of times we spent together chatting while I was working in the kitchen. Knowing that not all children communicate so openly, I look back and consider this an extra blessing.

Garrett loved to be involved in all sorts of extracurricular activities. I was constantly driving him to ball games, the home of a friend, and scouting activities. I especially enjoyed seeing the pleasure he found in being part of a team. I will always appreciate the efforts of the many coaches, teachers, and scoutmasters who made Garrett feel important and loved him for who he was.

Garrett was a child who had so much faith and a keen sense of right and wrong. There are lessons I will never forget that I learned from my son who had so much time for everyone around him.

Not many of us can look back on relationships cut short without regrets. Thankfully, the circumstances of our time together fostered happy memories and a deep love. I can only imagine the extra burden I would feel if I had to look back at things I wished I had been able to do for Garrett or words that had gone unspoken.

Sometimes I find myself wondering why this tragic trial had to come to someone as good as Garrett. Perhaps he came to us for a special reason and now we are expected to find ways to keep his goodness alive. Sadly, I know Garrett is not the only young person struggling with mental illness. Yes, his was a private struggle disguised in an incredibly handsome young man, who appeared so normal and happy. What I now know is that poor mental health is lethal and there are so many out there who we need to find and save. Mental health is treatable and suicide is preventable.

Had we known of Garrett's illness earlier, I believe our son's story would have had a very different ending. This is why I have found the courage to speak publicly to help remove the stigma associated with mental illness and to work to find more help for those in need. Like Gordon, I have become a strong advocate for mental-health screening. I was always diligent with yearly medical, dental, and eye exams for Garrett, but I never had a clue until it was too late that we faced a much more serious problem—one that could have been detected with something as simple as a TeenScreen. Now all I can do is to work to help save someone else's child. More information about TeenScreen and other mental health programs and organizations can be found in the resources guide at the end of this book. I would urge all parents who are concerned about their child's mental health to review the symptoms, risk factors, and warning signs listed there.

There are many occasions when I am speaking publicly, consoling another suicide survivor, or just doing routine activities that I feel that my dear Garrett is smiling down at me from Heaven above. Likewise, I know that Garrett is very proud of his father for writing this book—to encourage other families to be more vigilant in safeguarding the mental health of their children and to remind them that mental-health struggles aren't always obvious, that they don't always come clearly packaged in odd behavior or acting out. I also have faith that when Gordon's and my time here on earth is complete, we will once again be together with Garrett.

Yes, there are still times of grief, but most of all I just miss him. Like Gordon, I have found the value of trying to replace grief with gratitude whenever I think of Garrett. I am so grateful that I was blessed to be his mom, grateful that God placed Garrett with us, and grateful that he always made me feel so loved and wanted. I have twenty-two years of happy times filling my treasure chest of loving memories. What more could a mother ask for?

March 2006

REMEMBERING GARRETT

Garrett was more than my brother, he was my best friend for twenty-two years. He was always looking out for me, always available with a shoulder to lean on, an ear to listen, and a heart to understand. He was my source of strength through difficult days. I wish I had been there for him during his darkest days. I wish I had known how hard he was struggling.

—Brittany Anne Smith

Garrett was my big brother and, because he was seven years older, he seemed especially big. But he didn't tease me too much, and he set a good example. I miss his gentle presence.

—Morgan Smith

Garrett had such a big heart. It was as if he could understand exactly what others were going through and he always wanted to help in some way. When we were little, he used to tell me how when we grew up, he was going to do everything he could to help other people who were less fortunate than him. He would tell stories with great joy of how he would give homes to the homeless, feed the poor, find families for foster children, and perform many other acts of mercy and kindness. He had more love for others than I had ever seen in any of my other peers.

—Chris Leonard, childhood friend

The thing we loved most about Garrett was his kind heart. He loved everyone and pretty much everything. There was nothing shallow or phony about Garrett. He was sincere and caring. We always knew Garrett loved us.

—Dan and Liz Leonard, parents of Chris

When I think of Garrett Smith, the first image that comes to my mind is his infectious grin. It was quick, sincere, and heartwarming. His powerful build belied his gentle nature. He loved others completely and was firecely loyal to his friends. He was always grateful for kindnesses extended to him and quick with a thank you—always accompanied with that grin. I miss him.

—Kelly Brown, family friend

I can always remember Garrett worrying about others rather than himself. We spent a few nights just talking about other people and how we could help them. To see Garrett's love for others and selflessness really helped me.

—Sean Dubois, college friend

Unique, sweet, caring, compassionate, gentle, loving, dedicated, silly, and thoughtful are a few words that describe what Garrett was like, but unless you knew him you can never fully understand what an amazing person he was. When I was sad he would be there to cheer me up. When I was upset he was there to calm me down. He was always giving to others while trying to find happiness with himself.

—Sara Swan, college friend

I was not only shocked but devastated when I was told that Garrett had taken his life. How could I have missed Garrett's sadness and depression? I guess that, like thousands of others, Garrett suffered in silence and bravely put a smile on his face when he engaged others, so as not to burden them with his problems.

—Carol Ewen, friend and neighbor

We weren't here for him, but rather he was here for us. His loyalty as my friend is unmatched.

—Ethan Brown, best friend

RESOURCES

Sharon and I received literally thousands of phone calls and letters in the weeks and months following Garrett's death. We were touched to discover that so many people were keeping us in their thoughts and prayers. What we found most remarkable, however, was the number of individuals who wanted us to know that they or a family member had battled depression or bipolar illness.

We knew, of course, that Garrett was not alone in his struggle, but until those calls and letters poured in, I don't think we really grasped just how many families understood on a very personal basis what we were going through. Since Garrett's death, Sharon and I have met and talked with countless individuals and organizations that advocate on behalf of those suffering from mental illness or depression and who are working to prevent youth suicide. Many of these individuals and organizations were very helpful in the effort to pass the Garrett Lee Smith Memorial Act, and for that we will always be grateful.

Sharon and I remember Garrett each and every day. And we also remember the pledge we made to bring some good out of our son's tragic death. The Garrett Lee Smith Memorial Act was just the beginning in our fulfillment of that pledge. Mental-health issues will remain a priority of mine for as long as I serve in the Senate, and Sharon and I will continue to search for ways to increase awareness of the dangers that depression and bipolar illness pose to America's youth. In the pages that follow, we list some information we have found enlightening, and some resources that might be helpful.

Facts and Figures

- Suicide takes the lives of more than 30,000 Americans every year.

- Every eighteen minutes another life is lost to suicide.

- Between 1952 and 1995, the incidence of suicide among adolescents nearly tripled.

- Suicide is the third leading cause of death in the United States for those ages fifteen to twenty-four.

- Suicide is the second leading cause of death among college students.

- More teenagers and young adults die from suicide than from all medical illnesses combined.

- There are an estimated eight to twenty-five attempted suicides for each suicide death.

- Estimates are that only one third of teens at risk for suicide and one fifth of those with depression ever receive treatment.

- An estimated 2 to 15 percent of persons who have been diagnosed with major depression die by suicide. An estimated 3 to 20 percent of persons who have been diagnosed with bipolar disorder die by suicide.

- Between 40 and 60 percent of those who die by suicide are intoxicated at the time of death.

Symptoms of Major Depression

Unlike normal emotional experiences of sadness, loss, or passing mood states, major depression is persistent and can significantly interfere with an individual's thoughts, behavior, mood, activity, and physical health. Among all medical illnesses, major depression is the leading cause of disability in the United States and most other developed countries. According to the National Alliance for the Mentally Ill, the symptoms of depression include:

- Persistently sad or irritable mood

- Difficulty falling or staying asleep

- Pronounced change in appetite and energy

- Difficulty thinking, concentrating, and remembering

- Physical slowing or agitation

- Lack of interest in or pleasure from activities that were once enjoyed

- Feelings of guilt, worthlessness, hopelessness, or emptiness

- Excessive aggression and rage

- Presence of anxiety

- Excessive impulsivity

- Recurrent thoughts of death or suicide

- Persistent physical symptoms that do not respond to treatment, such as headaches, digestive disorders, and chronic pain

When several of these symptoms of depressive disorder occur at the same time, last longer than two weeks, or interfere with ordinary functioning, professional treatment may be needed.

Risk Factors of Youth Suicide

Young people intending to take their own life can be hard to identify, but specific risk factors do exist. According to the American Academy of Pediatrics, these can include:

- Talking openly about taking their own life

- A history of depression

- Family history of psychiatric disorders

- Disruption in the family

- Chronic physical or psychiatric illness

- Alcohol or drug use

Warning Signs of Youth Suicide

Experts have identified some common warning signs of suicide, which when acted upon can save lives. These signs include:

- Talking openly about committing suicide

- Expressing feelings regarding an inability to stop the pain or sadness, or to see a future without pain or sadness, or that they can't see themselves as worthwhile individuals

- Trouble eating or sleeping

- Drastic changes in behavior

- Withdrawal from friends and/or social activities

- Loss of interest in hobbies, work, school, etc.

- Giving away prized possessions

- Taking unnecessary risks

- Loss of interest in grooming or personal appearance

- Increased use of alcohol or drugs

How to Help

If a friend or loved one is threatening suicide, there are a number of ways in which to be of help:

- Be direct. Talk openly and matter-of-factly about suicide.

- Be willing to listen. Allow expressions of feelings. Accept the feelings.

- Convey the message that depression is real, common, and treatable.

- Get involved. Become available. Show interest and support.

- Don't be sworn to secrecy. Seek support.

- Take action. Remove the means of suicide, such as guns or stockpiled pills.

- Get help from persons or agencies that specialize in crisis intervention and suicide prevention.

Organizations That Can Help

ACTIVE MINDS
www.activemindsoncampus.org

A student-run mental-health awareness, education, and advocacy organization, whose mission is to utilize peer outreach to increase students' awareness of mental-health issues, provide information and resources about mental health and mental illness, encourage students to seek help as soon as it is needed, and to serve as liaison between students and the mental-health community.

AMERICAN FOUNDATION FOR SUICIDE PREVENTION
www.afsp.org

Supports research projects that help advance the understanding and treatment of depression and the prevention of suicide.

COLUMBIA UNIVERSITY TEENSCREEN PROGRAM
www.teenscreen.org

Of the many outstanding and life-saving programs offered to youth who are experiencing depression or thoughts about suicide, Sharon and I have been most impressed by TeenScreen, whose goal is to ensure that all parents are offered the opportunity for their teens to receive a voluntary mental-health checkup. The program's primary objective is to help young people and their parents through the early identification of mental health problems, such as depression, Parents of youth found to be at possible risk are notified and helped with identifying and connecting to local mental-health services where they can obtain further evaluation. No child is screened without parental consent. The results of the screen are confidential. Mental-health screening can take place in school, at doctors' offices, clinics, youth groups, shelters, and other youth-serving organizations and settings.

DEPRESSION AND BIPOLAR SUPPORT ALLIANCE
www.dbsalliance.org

A patient-directed organization that focuses on depression and bipolar illness and supports research to promote more timely diagnosis, develop more effective and tolerable treatments, and discover a cure. The organization fosters an understanding about the impact and management of these life-threatening illnesses by providing up-to-date, scientifically based tools and information written in language the general public can understand.

THE JASON FOUNDATION
www.jasonfoundation.com

The Foundation's mission is to promote awareness of and the prevention of teen suicide. It provides information and educational materials to youth, parents, and educators. Their school-based curriculum can be found in forty-seven states.

JED FOUNDATION/ULIFELINE
www.jedfoundation.org or www.ulifeline.org

Established by Phil and Donna Satow after the suicide of their son, Jed, a college sophomore, the Foundation's mission is to prevent suicide on college campuses and focus on the underlying causes of suicide. Its Web site includes links to counseling and health centers at colleges and universities across the country, as well as a list of services that experts consider essential for a good mental-health counseling center.

One of the Foundation's innovative programs is the Web site Ulifeline, an anonymous resource that provides students with a nonthreatening and supportive link to their college mental-health or counseling center, and helps them address such issues as depression, stress, and the pressures of college life. The site includes extensive information about mental health and an interactive screening tool to help students determine whether they or a friend are at risk.

NATIONAL ALLIANCE FOR THE MENTALLY ILL
www.nami.org

A nonprofit, grassroots, self-help support and advocacy organization composed of mental health-care consumers, families, and friends of people with severe mental illnesses. NAMI supports equitable services and treatment for the more than 15 million Americans with mental illness and their families.

NATIONAL COUNCIL FOR SUICIDE PREVENTION
www.ncsp.org

A clearinghouse for information on suicide prevention.

United States Senator Gordon H. Smith

NATIONAL HOPELINE NETWORK
www.hopeline.com

Provides individuals in suicidal crisis access to trained telephone counselors 24/7. It can be reached by calling 1-800-SUICIDE (784-2433).

NATIONAL SUICIDE PREVENTION LIFELINE
www.suicidepreventionlifeline.org

Provides immediate assistance to individuals in suicidal crisis by connecting them to the nearest available suicide prevention and mental-health service provider through a toll-free telephone number: 1-800-273-TALK (8255). This number can be reached 24/7. The Lifeline is the only national suicide prevention and intervention telephone resource funded by the federal government.

SUICIDE PREVENTION ACTION NETWORK
www.spanusa.org

The Network, created to help advance, implement, and evaluate a national strategy to address suicide, is the nation's only organization dedicated to leveraging grassroots support among suicide survivors (those who have lost a loved one to suicide) and others to advance public policies that will help prevent suicide.

SUBSTANCE ABUSE AND MENTAL HEALTH SERVICES ADMINISTRATION OF THE UNITED STATES DEPARTMENT OF HEALTH AND HUMAN SERVICES (SAMHSA)
www.samhsa.gov

An outstanding government organization that has launched a National Suicide Prevention Initiative and a National Strategy for Suicide Prevention (NSSP), representing the best combined work of advocates, clinicians, researchers, and suicide survivors. The NSSP lays out a framework for action to prevent suicide and guides development of an array of services and programs designed to transform attitudes and policies regarding suicide.

GARRETT LEE SMITH GRANTS

On September 20, 2005, the first grants established by the Garrett Lee Smith Memorial Act were awarded by the Substance Abuse and Mental Health Services Administration. Thirty-seven grants, totaling $9.7 million, will fund three areas of suicide prevention: state-sponsored suicide prevention and intervention initiatives for youth, suicide prevention efforts for college campuses, and a national suicide prevention resource center.

The following agencies received grants of up to $400,000 per year:

Arizona Department of Health Services

Commonwealth of Massachusetts
Maine Youth Suicide Prevention Program

Missouri Department of Mental Health

Montana Department of Public Health
and Human Services

Native American Rehabilitation Association
of the Northwest

Nevada Department of Health Services

NAMI of New Hampshire

New Mexico Department of Health

New York State Psychiatric Institute

Oklahoma Department of Mental Health

Tennessee Department of Mental Health

Texas Department of State Health Services

Virginia Department of Health

The Campus Suicide Prevention Grants will provide funding to twenty-two colleges and universities to improve services for students with mental-health problems. The following institutions received grants of up to $75,000 per year:

Arizona State University

Blue Mountain Community College

Columbia College

Daytona Beach Community College

George Washington University

Howard University

Johns Hopkins University

Keene State College

Northeastern Illinois University

Northwest Missouri State University

Pace University

Rensselaer Polytechnic Institute

Research Foundation of the

State University of New York

South Dakota School of Mines and Technology

Syracuse University

University of California, Irvine

University of California, Berkeley

University of Guam

University of North Carolina

University of Oregon

University of Wisconsin

Vanderbilt University

A Suicide Prevention Resource Center Grant of $2.6 million was also awarded to the Education Development Center, in Newton, Massachusetts. This grant will fund a national technical assistance center designed to provide guidance to states, territories, tribes, local communities, and other Garrett Lee Smith Memorial Act grantees to aid in their efforts to develop, implement, and evaluate suicide prevention programs.

ACKNOWLEDGMENTS

I have written many articles and editorials in my life, but never a book. I confess that it took many months to be comfortable writing a book about Garrett's life and death, and how his tragedy changed my life and my service as a United States Senator. The pain and poignancy of it all caused my courage to shrink. But time and the encouragement of a few close friends renewed my capacity to write. And while overwhelming emotions cut short many a writing session, I have found the telling of Garrett's story to be a healing experience, and I hope that other families will find solace and strength in these pages.

I owe a special mention of sincere gratitude to four people. First and foremost is my wife, Sharon. She is my faithful companion and a woman for all seasons. She gave me the time and the solitude necessary to write and, throughout, proved a reservoir of memory for insightful details.

Second is Kerry Tymchuk, a true friend who serves as my Oregon state director. He was the first to tell me that my memories of Garrett were the basis for an important book and he has been with me from the first page to the last, offering suggestions, corrections, and skillful edits.

It is Kerry who connected me with Mel Berger at the William Morris Agency. I am grateful to Mel for believing in this book, and for placing it in the care of Will Balliett at Carroll & Graf. I regarded Will as a friend from the first moment we met and know that this book was greatly improved by his intelligence, integrity, and insights.

ABOUT THE AUTHOR

Gordon H. Smith is currently serving his second term in the United States Senate, where he has represented his home state of Oregon since 1997. During his service in the Capitol, he has earned a reputation for independence, effectiveness, and an ability to bridge partisan differences. A graduate of Brigham Young University and Southwestern University School of Law, Smith entered politics after a successful career in the food processing industry.

The death of their son, Garrett, propelled Smith and his wife Sharon to embark on a mission to improve mental health programs and to combat the epidemic of youth suicide.